SELLING
WITH DIGNITY

Selling with Dignity
Copyright © 2021
by Harry Spaight

Printed and Electronic Versions
ISBN 978-956353-00-6
eBook ISBN 978-1-956353-02-0

(Harry Spaight / Motivation Champs)

To order additional copies or bulk order contact the publisher,
Motivation Champs Publishing.
www.motivationchamps.com

3/28/22

Anssy,

It was great to reconnect this past week. Glad to hear that you are doing well my friend!

I hope you enjoy the book.

SERVE FIRST
The Selling Will Follow!

Hanry

Endorsements

"Whether you are considering a career in sales or have been in the sales profession for decades you are going to love this book. You can sell with dignity. Harry will show you how. This is a step-by-step playbook that will encourage, inspire, and equip you to sell more and find fulfillment as you do."

Darrell Amy, Author of Revenue Growth Engine: How To Align Sales & Marketing to Accelerate Growth

Harry Spaight is one of the most inspiring people I know. He has a way of connecting with people that is raw and powerful. And he has not only brought a massive amount of value to my life, he has impacted my very existence. His new book, Selling With Dignity, will have the exact same effect on so many that pick it up and read. If you're looking for a sales book that endorses selling with honor and integrity, this is the book for you.

Dale Dupree, CEO of The Sales Rebellion

"Harry Spaight is an amazing individual! Above that, he is one who sells with dignity and always goes above and beyond for his clients. I highly recommend his new book *Selling With Dignity* and that you hire Harry to increase your sales and profitability."

Daniel Gomez, Keynote Speaker, Executive Speaker, Corporate Trainer, Award-Winning Business Coach

"*Selling With Dignity* is not just a fad, it's a philosophy that will ensure sales professionals build incredible relationships, help many people, and earn a great amount of income. I've had the unique opportunity to work with Harry and see him selling with dignity since 2009. I can easily say that there isn't another person who can build rapport and gain trust with his clients as fast as Harry does, and that's a huge part of being successful in sales. I've seen people not buy from Harry, but refer him to their friends. I've witnessed people pay more than they could have, just to do business with Harry and his teammates. And I've experienced Harry doing the right thing for his clients when it was easier not to. He understands what it means to love people and have their best interests in mind. He knows how to be successful, and it's all laid out in this book."

Eric Konovalov, Author of B2B Sales Secrets and Co-Host of Lead Sell Grow - The Human Experience Podcast

"Harry Spaight delivers brilliant and timeless knowledge on how to optimize your mindset as well as your sales skills in *Selling With Dignity*. The approach is not only more enjoyable, it also produces the highest levels of success. It is packed with valuable advice around psychology, communication styles, how to banish self-limiting thoughts and how to be the best human being you can be. Being a better person will make you a better salesperson and you will find joy in both. Two huge thumbs up!"

James Muir, Founder & CEO of Best Practice International

"Harry Spaight takes living through relationship-building to a level few will ever achieve. In an age where technology is overly treasured, Harry's book will convince you that being genuine, trustworthy, and kind will be immensely more rewarding."

Stephen Rolla, Senior Partner Pros Elite Group

"*Selling With Dignity* is spot-on! Treating your prospect with dignity is not only the best sales approach...it should be your ONLY 'go-to' sales approach. Providing your solutions with honor and respect is the way to create happy, long-term customers that come back for years to come."

Scott Schilling, Executive Coach, International Trainer & Speaker, Vice President of Strategic Partnerships

"Harry preaches and teaches that sales is a noble profession and should be driven by a love for people and a genuine concern and care for others. (Can I get an Amen?) In *Selling with Dignity*, Harry dismantles the outdated sales mindset and methods that no longer support and serve today's modern professionals. Harry dives into the skills that *all* professionals need today to be successful and thrive in the new business environment. His book is informative, engaging, and filled with ideas and insight into the respectable and fun world of sales."

Liz Wendling, President of Insight Business Consultants and Author of The Heart of Authentic Selling

"If you are looking to increase your sales make sure you pick up a copy of *Selling With Dignity*. In this book Harry will show you not only how to sell with dignity, but more importantly how to build lasting relationships. Make sure you take notes, but more importantly make sure you apply these incredible tactics so you can succeed not only in sales, but also in life."

Christopher J. Wirth, Speaker, Trainer, Mental Performance Coach and Author of "The Positivity Tribe" and the host of the No Quit Living Podcast

"How can a sales job become a fulfilling sales career? How can we develop our personal sales brand in such a way that clients trust us and refer their own contacts to us? How does one succeed in sales and still sleep well at night? *Selling With Dignity* will show you how Harry did exactly that and how you can, too. By sharing timeless nuggets of wisdom and many firsthand stories of what the day-to-day sales world is like, this book is a blueprint for honing your craft."

Curtis Ziemba, Professional Educator-Sales Cox Communications

Dedication

To my wife Kathleen, thank you for living the dream with me. The journey with you never gets old.

To Audrey, Harrison, and Shepard, you inspire me to be the best I can be. As Napoleon Hill said "Whatever your mind can conceive and believe, it can achieve." Pursue your dreams throughout your entire life.

To all those who would like to succeed in sales without compromising your values, this is for you. Selling in a dignified way will result in tremendous relationships and rich financial rewards.

Acknowledgments

A hearty thank you goes out to all of my collaborators and encouragers. You have helped me to put into writing these core values that I hope will be of immense value to those that read this book.

Contents

Foreword

There is a well-known poem by an anonymous author, entitled, *"People always come into your life for a reason, a season, or a lifetime."* When you figure out which it is, you know exactly what to do.

I am a firm believer that people come into your life for a reason. Some may call it intuition, some may call it being at the right place at the right time or some may call it pure luck.

In this crazy, busy world we live in today which is digitally driven, socially connected, and mobile empowered, we have the opportunity to meet and connect with people in many different ways.

That being said, Harry Spaight and I connected via LinkedIn on April 1, 2016. And at that moment in time, neither of us realized the profound impact we would have on each other, our journey, and our lives.

In bringing Selling from the Heart, the book, and the podcast, to the forefront; I didn't realize the movement and impact this would create within the sales world. It became crystal clear, this is what brought Harry and I together in a deep and meaningful way.

I believe relationships are built, nurtured, and strengthened at the heart level. They are further nourished through honor and dignity.

What a privilege and blessing to write the foreword to *Selling with Dignity.*

We've all heard the old saying, "like attracts like". This unequivocally applies to my deep and personal relationship with Harry Spaight. Relationships flourish based upon conversations, intentional curiosity, and a sincere desire to truly leave someone in a better state of being.

The more conversations I had with Harry, the more I was drawn to Harry. The more I kept wanting more. What I admire about Harry is his giving and servant mindset. Spend a few minutes and you will soon find this to be true.

I am a firm believer that in order to give one must lead with a helping hand. Harry learned this first hand through his decades of missionary work which he then transferred over into sales.

Dignity, the state or quality of being worthy of honor or respect.

So, how do salespeople in a post-trust sales world, where many buyers are skeptical and leery of them become respected? They sell with honor, dignity and carry themselves with high degrees of professionalism.

In reading *Selling with Dignity*, you will soon start to uncover that Harry is giving himself to you. Harry has created and provided the roadmap to what I believe is the holy grail within sales… selling with honor and dignity. It's about giving, serving, and leading with your heart.

You will discover **Selling with Dignity**

Does not mean manipulating customers into giving you money.

Does not mean you lead with deception

Does not mean that you relentlessly haggle people until they give in.

Rather Selling with Dignity means

You intentionally listen to your buyers' needs and guide them to the best solution to their problems.

You genuinely care about others and connect them to your

product/service because you are confident that what you do makes a difference.

Your genuine belief in yourself and what you do is so contagious that you inspire others into taking action.

Selling is an honorable profession. What takes it to the next level is when it is done right, done with respect, care, and a giving heart.

In 1936, Dale Carnegie wrote one of the all-time classics, *How To Win Friends and Influence People*. I believe the core foundation of the book lies within *Selling with Dignity*, it is about building relationships and changing the way people think.

This can all be accomplished by treating today's buyers and your clients with dignity and respect. Honor, cherish, and value who they are and not for what they may buy from you.

As Harry refers to throughout his book, selling is as fundamental as buying. I encourage all those in sales to apply the principles within this book to bring honor and dignity back into selling.

I can't possibly stress enough the importance of leading your life with dignity, honor, and respect. Apply this to your sales career and you will transform your relationships with your clients, and isn't this what you crave?

Selling with Dignity is a lifestyle.

Larry Levine
Author of "Selling from the Heart, How Your Authentic Self Sells You."

Introduction

I was clearly the one that stood out as different. It wasn't just about the age either as I was starting this new adventure at age thirty-five. I was in the middle of what was referred to as a sales bullpen. Rows of three tiny cubicles that were probably thirty inches wide without any dividers. There was no room to speak of. If you rolled the chair back one would bump into the person behind them. The only divider was the barrier that started at the desk. In this bullpen were young men, recent college grads with their pressed white shirts and ties getting their start in the competitive market of selling copiers. I was getting started myself but I had some catching up to do being ten to twelve years older than most. Even my manager was considerably younger. I felt like an old man who would be learning from the kids. Sort of like asking your own kid to show you how to use a feature on your smartphone. But this would be more complicated than that. If I was ten years younger, I would still be older than the majority. If they were ten years younger, they would have been in eighth grade! Talk about an age gap!

A few months prior I was riding around on dirt roads on my little motorcycle with my wife, serving others doing mission work in a third-world country, the Dominican Republic. I was there to help others, to serve people, and make my small contribution in life. Picture a person carrying around a Bible visiting others, helping with the building of churches, speaking from the stage, or helping people make some serious life changes. That was me for the previous fifteen years. I was comfortable in that world.

Now here I was, seemingly light-years away and sitting in my new very different surroundings. There was no privacy, no quiet conversations, it was all out in the open. I heard too many "private" conversations in hush tones that were heard by the other eight people nearby. There was no coming and going as I pleased, there were clocks and regular working hours and of course, a manager nearby to keep an eye on what people were doing. I can tell you, for this free spirit, this was definitely going to require some serious adjusting. One was my immediate group of peers. Their conversations were about sports, girls, all alcohol-laced with some adjectives that I hadn't really heard since I was a teenager in high school. My former peers in the mission work were people that never cursed. Our "curses" were words like fudge, shoot, darn, and crap. If I was one that was offended by cursing, I wouldn't have lasted an hour.

Despite needing to adjust to the new very different surroundings, I also needed to learn. I knew squa-doodle (non-technical term for being clueless) about business and technology. I would be calling on businesses and people who would be recognized by titles like IT Director, IS managers, MIS, CFOs, CTOs, and Creative Directors. I needed to find out what each of these was and what their challenges were too. Additionally, I had to learn about the actual product I was selling. In my case, it was color printers that ranged in price from about $15,000 US and up to about $60,000. We are talking about the 90s here. This was going to be a challenging road.

My favorite sales book I had read up to this was *The Greatest Salesman in the World*. When I read it, it was totally relatable. Service to others and bringing love to people were values that I had. Would love and service to others supersede knowledge? I had plenty of love and knew how to serve and I knew the value of learning in order to improve. Learning would be critical.

What drove me to want to do well? I think a sense of pride may have had something to do with it. There was potential for failing in this endeavor but it certainly was not going to be due to lack of effort. I was the type of person who had a pretty solid work ethic. I was not driven by money or prestige. Having been relatively poor financially in the mission lifestyle, making any money where I didn't have to clean bathrooms or climb on ladders again would be a win. I simply wanted to provide for my wife and future children. I honestly had no idea as to how much income potential there was. My eyes were definitely going to be opened about income over the next couple of years.

How would my values fit in? Servant-mindedness, honesty, integrity, trustworthiness, humility, tactful humor, and love were values that I had been working on for most of my adult life. It wasn't long before I started seeing some different values that I felt like I needed to avoid. In particular was the self-centeredness and willingness to bend the truth, especially in competitive situations. I was not one who was going to do things that appeared slimy. If a buyer was going to choose to go with a competitor, I did not look at that as a situation where I needed to beg and plead for the business with some pressure tactic or by dropping my price dramatically to get the business.

I felt I could bring a little more dignity into selling. After all, I was probably the only former missionary in sales in the region. That would be my differentiator, my identity. I may not have known much about business and I had tons of learning ahead of me, but I knew how to serve and take care of people. That is where dignity came in. Keep it above board.

I could serve with the best and that was the path I would take. I had all of the training from the mission work. Our guidebook was none other than the Good Book really. From that training on how to live and treat others was the guide that I could use in business I thought. I was not alone. The more I read and listened to sales gurus like Tom Hopkins, Brian Tracy, and Earl Nightingale, I heard or saw principles that were written long ago.

While there are people who are well-intentioned giving their tips about sales and techniques about closing business or that sales is just a numbers game and one can make a quick buck if they follow their steps exactly. That is not what you will find on these pages. I have watched a number of sales trainers come and go and wondered did they ever sell anything other than the company president as to how awesome their training was? I think the main differentiator for me is the fact that I lived these principles in a highly competitive industry for over twenty years. These are not philosophical ideas, they are tried and true practices that have worked to the benefit of the client and the seller.

To help better understand just how well these principles and selling with dignity worked in my career, I would like to share a little from my past. First of all, in supporting my mission life, I had a small janitorial/maintenance business. Our income bracket was in the very low category, well below the median income nationally in the USA. The career choice up until then was all about helping people and the income that resulted from that was not the priority in life. So we lived frugally and made the most of what we earned. We rented inexpensive apartments and honestly never thought about buying a home. We dealt with mice and can even share a story about chasing one with a hockey stick in our kitchen but I will spare the details! One place we had for about a year lacked a sink in the bathroom. It was either the faucet in the tub or the kitchen sink for choices in our very modest three-room apartment. The idea of raising a family and living a better lifestyle seemed to be out of reach. Then things started to change.

What led to the change? It was finding the right sales opportunity. In my first year in sales, I made more of an income than any of the years that my small janitorial business earned. I finally reached the average median income and then proceeded to pass that and never look back. In my third year in sales, I was recognized as one of the top ten individuals out of hundreds in the country if not thousands. Shortly after that, I was recognized again for similar successes. Getting rewarded with all-inclusive trips and staying at exclusive five-star hotels was a completely different and much better experience than what my janitorial business and lifestyle permitted.

In just a few years we went from a three-room apartment into a three-bedroom home with our growing little family. Then we upgraded that home to the home of our dreams in a gated golf course community with a wooded back lot with a stream that our children spent countless hours playing in the mud or searching for crawfish and just living the kid's dream. Instead of buying cars with tons of miles on them, we actually for the first time in our lives went to car dealerships to pick out the new SUV. It was a totally different set of circumstances that we now experienced, all due to this concept of selling with dignity.

Shortly after those successful years, I was promoted to a position of sales leadership and eventually became the branch manager for the company's Washington DC office located just a few blocks from the White House. Many who are in positions of sales managers have to become "closers" for their team. That was not my style to be the high-pressured closer. I did help bring in the business by treating people well and periodically I did make calls to see where people stood and to understand their time frame. I did this without resorting to compromising tactics. From there I was promoted to Vice President of Sales. All along the way, I was serving others and putting these valuable principles into practice.

The lifestyle economically was a completely different path compared to the one I was on. Like I mentioned about lacking business acumen, I also lacked an understanding of the income potential that a career in sales could offer. Not that money is the only pursuit in life, it does make the ability to have better choices. Having the ability to live in great neighborhoods with security and giving my wife the freedom to stay at home to raise children as well. All of this was due to putting into practice what I learned in the mission life and continually sharpening the skills related to selling and understanding people.

The purpose of this book is pretty simple. Sales does not have to be dirty or slimy or uncomfortable. If you are doing something that feels dirty, let's figure out how to reach the goal and always stay above board. I am far from perfect. I have tried a few things over the years and felt slimy myself and said that is not who I am or what I want to be like and decided to stay away from those paths. There are many who want to be salespeople or are business owners or solopreneurs that desire to be better at the craft of selling but may only hear about closing or pressure tactics that are not appealing for them. My goal is to help you and to restore some honor and dignity with this age-old profession. It can be done. I have been doing it for decades and sleep very well at night.

Sales is a noble profession. One of my favorite compliments is when buyers would tell me "What I like about you is that you don't act like a salesperson. You are just a regular person and treat me like a person". Think about that. Many view the idea of acting like a salesperson as a real negative. So it is time to change this sentiment. You may recognize that each chapter is based on a principle that is found in the Good Book. I lived by this Book in mission life for about fifteen years. The principles are timeless and powerful. They work in business as they do in our personal lives. Like many of the greats, I believe Sales should have a love for others as a motivating force. Ask any salesperson what they like about sales, if they say the money, then they are missing the point. It should be about helping others. The money will follow. If you like helping others, solving problems, showing love to all kinds of people, then you can be successful too. Join the Selling With Dignity movement; it's the only way!

Section 1
Finding Your Voice

CHAPTER 1

Selling With Dignity ~ It Works

"Treat those around you with respect and dignity
and they will thrive." ~Richard Branson

Why the question of selling with dignity? Is it worth discussing? Richard Branson certainly believes in its value and I don't imagine that any would argue against his success over the decades. You have heard on numerous occasions that we are all "in sales." Yet some of us are still uneasy about selling. It is obvious that many do not care about the dignity of others in sales or of their own self-dignity. Some businesses are anything but dignified when it comes to their practices of taking advantage of the elderly or un-informed. We may have those nightmares about the worst sales experiences of our lives, imagined or real. We know what we don't want to be like so we choose not to sell at all. Why the fear? Many dread being viewed as the sleazy, money-hungry, self-serving types that have infiltrated the business of sales over the years.

Sales for some is a scene right out of a movie. Imagine making the "mistake" of pulling into a used car dealership because the shiny late-model Acura caught your attention. You have been looking for this model and the price looks like it will save a small fortune. Your mind starts questioning what you just did. You know better. What were you thinking, driving into a used car lot?? You start to justify it. It can't be that bad. I have to get over my fears, you say. You give in to the temptation to get out for a closer look. You park the car kind of hidden behind other cars. Inconspicuously you walk towards the car but just as an antelope taking a sip of water in a refreshing oasis on the Serengeti (or the savanna) you dreadfully sense the early signs of danger approaching.

A lion…I mean a man, somewhat overweight approaches you wearing a loud plaid brown sport coat that hasn't fit since the last season of *Friends*, nicely accessorized with an unmatching red and black striped tie. Every stereotype of a "used car salesman" is nailed. *What was I thinking?* you ask. As he approaches the thought crosses your mind, "Can I run and get back to my car faster than this person can get any closer to me?" You look at the man, then your car, and back at the man, then the car trying to measure the speed required. Can you run like an antelope, like you did as a kid? The lion is too close and you surrender. Your last gasp of life is a memory of you driving into the car lot. Oops, the salesman is too close to make the escape. You shout at the man saying "I'm just looking!" hoping he will go away. No such luck. He is undeterred and on a mission. You after all represent his commission check. Nothing more. Nothing less. You are the dollar signs that he has his eyes set on.

As the man gets closer, you see his clothing looks like it was slept in. Crumpled slacks and jacket with what appears to be a yellow mustard stain on the faded gray, which once was a white shirt. The clothes reek from stale cigarette smoke. He bellows a scary loud "Hello! That one is a real beauty!" loud enough for someone that may be standing a hundred feet away. The greeting comes with a gush of warm air fragranced by the morning coffee that has soured the breath.

This is a bad dream but you can't wake up from it. You turn your head trying to hide your uneasiness of the stomach. He reaches out the hand, long fingernails make you think about vampire movies. Do you shake the hand or look at it? You choose to sheepishly hold out the hand in a fist as there is no way you are going to clasp on to the germ-ridden paw that is waiting before you while you pray that no disease will plague you for the rest of your life. Before asking anything he is already telling you how great the car is and it's too good of a deal to pass up. You know that you have to leave but he quickly maneuvers himself between you and the escape route back to your car. He sees you as a commission check slipping away. Desperately, he asks, "What can I do to get you into this car today?"

Is this the fear you have of what salespeople are really like? Although a profession that should be driven by love for people and genuine care for others, it has been corrupted with greed, lying, fraud, and a host of other unscrupulous traits and actions. If you dread buying a car or shopping for anything where a salesperson is involved, you probably experienced some of this in your life.

Because of this type of experience, we are on our guard. We question the motives of financial planners, insurance agents, realtors, car sales, attorneys, home remodelers, and now even some in healthcare where dentists, chiropractors, and physicians are selling *programs*. Do they really care about us or are they looking purely for the benefits for themselves? Are they solving a problem or trying to get you to buy and pay more than you desire? That is not always easy to determine. WE DO NOT NEED TO BE LIKE THIS!

Sales and Transactions Drive The Economic Engine

Now let's think about the good side of sales because there really is a good side. Honestly, there is! If you haven't thought it through, let's do that. Have you heard the expression that everything starts with a sale? It is true. Everything starts with a sale of something. Selling drives the economic engine. People buy "stuff". In order for that "stuff" to exist, it has to be produced, made, or grown generally speaking. That same stuff you buy also needs to be fixed or maintained or serviced or updated periodically, which means people service the "stuff" too. So we have the people that make, the people that sell, and the people that service stuff. We also have farmers who grow and sell food as well. Service industries that help with the quality of life are available for us too. Of course, we can't forget the banks that are lending money to help us to buy more stuff. From all the money that is flowing, taxes are collected and that tax revenue provides the money required to provide community services like building and maintaining bridges, roads, police, fire departments, schools, teachers, administrations, healthcare at times, government stimulus checks in times of need, defense, all of these community services and so much more than we have time to mention. All of these services and infrastructure come into existence and start with the sale of something. If people don't buy, then people don't make stuff and without buying and selling, jobs get cut, companies go out of business, farmers stop producing, the services start to slow down and tax revenues drop and bad things start to happen all around.

With the above in mind, do you see how selling is really doing good for your family, your company, your community, and your country? If you don't believe me, take a look at countries where the governments provided everything for people like the former

Soviet Union. That country, as large as it was, collapsed after only seventy-five years of existence. When the ability to produce and be rewarded financially is taken from people, those countries eventually face collapse or massive uprisings. Sales and the economic engine are a huge part of the progress that has been made throughout history.

This is where dignity and honor should be part of the fabric of selling. Selling is as fundamental as buying. There is no need for sales to be viewed as something less than honorable. *We can bring honor and dignity back into selling.* We can be the ones with whom people want to do business due to our honesty and genuine love for people. That is the purpose of this book. Simply to help sellers see that they can provide a special service to others with a clean conscience and know they are helping people and can sleep soundly every night while earning a nice living.

However, selling is not easy. If it were easy, then we would not have people leaving "sales" every day. Some small business owners know that it would be best for their business success to be sellers too. Yet many feel that they are not cut out for sales. They say they are not good at it. They are great at providing service and running their company but selling is best left to salespeople they think. In their minds, selling means to act like the stereotypical salesperson and that is not who they want to be.

Some who are in sales or need to sell are going to quit and say "This isn't for me," or "I tried and I just am not any good at it." It is one thing to test out something and decide that you don't like it. But sometimes with sales, people take opportunities that require them to act like some obnoxious pushy salesperson and that is where sales get a bad reputation, and we want nothing to do with that.

Some sales leaders will encourage their salespeople to compromise their ethical standards with what they call little "white lies." Tell them it does something when it doesn't or make promises that aren't kept. Those little white lies start to grow bigger and bigger. Once one goes down a path of telling untruths, it becomes easier and easier. Before long, anything that is spoken can be a lie. So that is how corrupt selling can begin. It starts with a "little" lie and then it progresses to bigger ones. Movies like Glengarry Glen Ross, The Boiler Room, The Wolf of Wall Street, Wall Street, and others make one think that selling is nothing but corrupt.

SIDEBAR

For an uplifting view of sales, *The Pursuit of Happyness* movie shows what the benefits of hard work and integrity can do for people who want to succeed as a good human in sales.

You May Just Need to Find The Right Fit

When I started years ago, the first opportunity I took was not a good one for me. I found myself in people's homes at night trying to sell insurance. Not that this is wrong by any stretch, I was uncomfortable with certain aspects of that and eventually found something that suited me better. I could have just quit sales altogether but finding the right environment where there was decent pay, good training, good leadership, and the fact I was calling on businesses, not the consumer, was what I needed in order to succeed.

If you are in sales now, are you finding it a challenge to blend in with other salespeople? Are you feeling like you aren't a strong closer, that you are not pushy enough or hungry enough? Are the traits of others in your office, ones that you admire? Are you assigned to a sales leader who does not seem to share your values and just wants numbers at all costs? Your answers may indicate that you are in the wrong place. Sometimes it is just a case of finding the right company and culture in order to find our sweet spot in sales.

If sales is not for you, don't fret. The world needs creative as well as task oriented people, designers, engineers, builders, doctors, nurses, EMTs, police, firefighters, accountants, scientists, teachers, manufacturers, services, the arts, and the like. Not everyone wants to be in sales and that is certainly fine. We are not trying to talk people into becoming salespeople.

Many of us are "people people". Everything we do is focused on people. We may have a servant's mind. We care about people. We like to help people. If someone asks, we are there to assist. Yet many of us do not feel like we are "cut out" for sales. Sales is for the extroverts, the smooth talkers, the ones who are thick-skinned, really outgoing types. That may be true for some, but certainly not all. Some of the best-sellers are those who are modest, humble, and empathetic listeners, even introverts can do very well. They sell, without losing their dignity.

What is your view of salespeople? Do you attribute the traits of honor, integrity, dignity, genuineness, friendliness, trustworthiness, care, love, generosity, patience, empathy to the people you know with whom you have had experience in the sales arena? Or do you feel that all salespeople are self-centered, obnoxious, egotistical, pushy, and impatient? Perhaps they start out really nice but once things don't go their way, they turn into a different person like the old Dr. Jekyll and Mr. Hyde story.

SWD MASTER TIP

Selling can absolutely be performed with dignity. Selling drives the economic engine. Just because there are some who are sleazy and act in a less than dignified way, that does not mean we all need to act that way. People who are humble, caring, introverted, and listeners are often the best salespeople. They are the ones who people say "I like you because you don't act like a salesperson!" Sellers with dignity rise to the top!

CHAPTER 2

Selling is Serving

"You can get everything you want in life if you will just help other people get what they want." ~Zig Ziglar

Think of your favorite server in a restaurant, one who is friendly and delights in providing excellent service with love for people, in exchange for a nice tip. Is the server selling? You may not think of the server as a salesperson but if they are offering specials, drinks, appetizers, desserts, and periodically asking how you are doing with your choices, they are indeed selling. Which type of server do you enjoy the most? Someone who is kind, caring, trustworthy with their recommendations, patient with your decision process, servant-minded, empathetic if something isn't as delicious as expected? Or do you want a person to just take your order, not show any interest in you personally, appearing that they are too busy to understand what you truly want, disappear after your meal comes, sigh heavily if you are unhappy with a meal, and then show up with the check? I would think the former rather than the latter.

I remember having a conversation with a salesperson on our team. He was struggling and clearly unhappy. While speaking through how we were helping people have better experiences in their jobs with what we were providing for them, the words that came out of his mouth stunned me. "I don't care about people, I am in this for the money!" Well, that was the problem. People see through us. We can't hide who we truly are. If we don't care about them, we are like the server in the restaurant who is there to serve but does not like serving. That person will not be successful over the long term. If you truly do not care about people and are in it for the money, this book probably won't be of much value. People will figure us out based on the vibes we are sending from our inner person. If we are looking at them as commission opportunities and not as real people with their own thoughts, values, needs, experiences, and challenges, they will figure us out and find a salesperson who actually cares about them.

Now, as a servant-minded person, what can help us to become better in the craft of selling? First of all, keep the servant-minded attitude. That is one of your core values and is a strength, not a weakness. Helping others get what they want as Zig said, is being servant-minded and it shows that this mindset will have its rewards too. I am not saying that you will be living in a twelve-bedroom house with the wealthy in Beverly Hills, but you can definitely carve out a very nice living. That quote is one that I kept in mind in my early years in sales especially.

What does this saying mean for those of us in sales? Simply serve others and the way you treat them will be returned to us. Instead of looking out for our own commission interests, serve and the results will follow. Does it work? Without a doubt, it works! It may not work overnight, but it will work in due time.

Picture the server in the upscale restaurant. Are they serving or selling? Are they doing both? They are "selling" beverages, appetizers, desserts, and highlighting the more expensive specials.

They know that it is likely the higher your bill will be, the better their commission. Yet when we order water instead of a glass of wine or pass on the dessert, they keep smiling and serving, treating us like royalty, without concern for their "commission". They are providing a service and a product (the nice meal) and are making sure we are pleased with everything. That is selling with dignity, just in a condensed format.

Selling is helping. Selling is serving. Selling is showing love for others. It is honorable and dignified. There are some bad apples but that has nothing to do with you. Showing others you truly care is all you need to do to separate yourself from the ones who care only about themselves. It really is pretty easy to do when you look at it this way.

People want to do business with people like you. They just don't know you yet or understand that you are servant-minded yet. How will they find out about you? They will not magically appear. We need to go find them. Where are our potential clients? Are they at work? Are they involved in a charity? Are they in our places of worship? Are they at our children's soccer game? Are they at network or Chamber events? No matter where they are if we are friendly and servant-minded, we can look for people who we can serve.

SWD MASTER TIP

Instead of saying "how can I help you?" use the phrase, "how may I serve you?" This great line was shared by Scott Schilling when he was on our Lead Sell Grow podcast. I think it's a great way to show that you are a servant-minded individual.

CHAPTER 3

Be A Giver

"Be of service to others. Only what you give can be multiplied back into your own life." – Mary Kay Ash

Who of us doesn't enjoy hearing about the person who leaves a $1,000 tip to a server for breakfast at the local Waffle House? For the person who gives generously, there isn't scorekeeping. There isn't any payback desired and many times these gifts are offered anonymously. When we expect something in return, it isn't really giving.

Givers Stop and Greet Others

What are some very simple actions that you can take that are absolutely free and go a long way towards making someone's day? A hello, a smile, a look in the eye, a question about them, their day, their family, their job, their weekend, their challenges, etc?

Treat the janitor like the CEO. This simply means that everyone is important and to treat people like they all have value. I can relate to this since I had my own janitorial office cleaning business to support myself and my wife when we were involved in the Mission activity. I mopped floors, emptied trash, washed windows and cleaned restrooms. It was all pretty humbling work. I did this work in order to spend my days in the mission activity. So by day, I was Mission Man. By night, I was Cleaning Guy. At times, there were people working late in the office, usually these would be someone at an executive level. I always enjoyed it when one would stop what they were doing, look at me and ask me "How was the weekend?", "How is business?" or "Why are you always smiling?" These questions wouldn't cost anything other than a couple of minutes of time. Yet they paid dividends. I always would work a little harder when someone showed a little warmth or appreciation. Asking people sincerely about them will help create relationships everywhere in life. Givers genuinely care about others.

Being a Giver at Networking and Chamber Events

As salespeople or business owners, it's fairly common to join Chambers of Commerce and networking groups. I was rarely a believer in these types of events until recent years. Yes, that was pretty foolish of me. I prejudged a bit thinking everyone who attended these was thinking "what's in it for me?" Part of the reason I had a negative attitude about these events was due to the way people handed out business cards and kept repeating their pitch to everyone.

Putting that aside, I have met some really phenomenal people at these events. People that are real givers and helpers are the ones that you will want to find in these events, especially if you are one that also is a giver and a helper. Start asking this question, "is there anything I can do for you?" Be sincere and pause. When others hear this, they will see that you truly do care about them and their success.

Most go into these networking events thinking about lead generation. It's all part of building your business. If our only goal is to build our business, then how will others view us? How much better would it be to go to these events with the mindset of being helpful towards others. We would build more relationships and friendships which in turn would lead to people giving us business referrals.

If you go into events trying to make a new friend or get to know someone without concern as to what the payback will be far better than going with the mindset of handing out twenty business cards. Imagine the reputation you will build if you show you care about everyone. People will be more inclined to recommend you if you are friendly and helpful than if you are viewed as a taker.

I remember going to an event where a person asked what I did. When I replied, they said something like, we probably aren't good for each other and walked away with a smile. I can tell you that whenever I saw the person at other events, I remembered that I was not worthy of a conversation. If you are conversing with one who may not be a great connection for you, spend a few minutes and ask them how their business is going and what they are doing to grow it. Show a little interest in the person as a human being, not just a lead generator for you.

Another common action is handing out business cards with a statement of "if you ever need or know someone that needs (fill in the blank with whatever you do or what you offer) please call me." My friend Bob, who does a lot of networking and is a true pro, described this technique as a "sprinkler". He related it to the water sprinkler that sprays water everywhere and he flipped business cards imitating the sprinkler. It definitely was a funny site and showed how silly it was to hand out cards without having genuine conversations. Those cards that have been sprinkled without real conversations, all end up in the trash bin.

There is another way we may show we are acting as a taker with networking events. This is the "skipper". This type says they are committed to attending and may even pay dues. They may go to events for a while and then start skipping meetings because they are too busy. They only show up when they have free time or when business is slow or just enough to hold their spot in the group. What is the "skipper" showing the group? It really is all about them and they are not bringing value to others. If you commit to a group, stay committed. A few hours per week is not going to jeopardize someone's business.

Saying we are too busy to attend is implying that others are not busy. It also implies that one will only attend when business is slow. In both cases, it is just the same as saying "I don't see any value in helping any of you at this event." For proof of this, I know of an excellent group of business owners that meets every week and has done so for nearly thirty years. Business owners are the ones that could justifiably use the "too busy" excuse to miss. However, they are incredibly dedicated to the schedule and everyone in that group gives leads to each other and acts like they are real friends with each other. These are the types of groups that will be successful in growing each other's business.

What if you have not ventured into the networking community? What is holding you back? Do you feel as I did once that the people are mostly takers? Or do you feel nervous and don't like to be in a room with a bunch of strangers? Maybe you aren't as confident as you could be. Do you see the benefit in participating in groups like this? If so, think as you are walking in or logging in to a virtual event, that you are going to have at least one good conversation and that you are going to help others. It will help overcome the fear. Helping others first is the right mindset for overcoming any feelings of self-doubt.

Be intentional. Look for events where there are decision-makers. Be a giver with people that can buy or recommend your service. This may include paying for the privilege of being in their company. Go where your buyers are. If they are at events that cost a little more than the general admission seating, pay the extra fee to be with them.

I once heard a speaker on a podcast talk about the butterflies she had before her speech. What she did to overcome the nervousness was simply think that she was speaking in order to help others. That thought helped her and it helped me as well when she shared it. So, whenever I get nervous about doing something, I think of the goal, which is to help others and make their lives a little better. That calms my nerves and puts the focus on others, not myself. This is the same with networking and going to an event the first time. After you meet one person, the next time there will be at least one person you know. Then two then four then six and before long, you will know a whole bunch of folks! It works!

Being a Giver With The Team

In many businesses, there are salespeople that interact with administrative people and support people. What do you think is the general view of salespeople in these environments? If you don't know, all you need to do is ask. Some may complain that salespeople are all about themselves. They think that salespeople have the easiest jobs and get paid the most. They also demand the most from the support team to fix the problems they sometimes cause. Hopefully, we are not acting like this and if we are perceived this way, can we do something to improve this outlook?

Typically, salespeople look at themselves as the ones keeping the company in business. After all, they are the ones driving sales. It is true, while nothing happens without a sale, the attitude of a salesperson sharing this sentiment and acting like a primadonna, is not one to build a good culture and feeling of teamwork. Wouldn't it be better to share how valuable the team is and that we need a team behind the scenes so *we all* can be successful?

SWD MASTER TIP

Being a Giver cannot be faked. Start doing things for others without any concern about getting a payoff in return. The real givers are not thinking about how they will be rewarded. They just give and care because that is their nature. There will be rewards but they aren't thinking about that. The giving mindset is what selling with dignity is all about.

CHAPTER 4

Who Says That Nice Guys Finish Last?

"Contrary to the cliche, genuinely nice guys most often finish first or very near it." ~Steve Forbes

"You are too nice."

"Sales is a dirty business and if you aren't like a pit bull, you won't succeed."

"There is a lot of swearing in the sales bullpen. I'm not sure someone like you could handle that. Nice people typically don't last in this business."

These were the statements coming from a hiring sales manager who was interviewing me for a sales opportunity. I first thought she was testing me to see if I would respond to her concerns. What brought up these concerns in the first place?

When asked what my qualifications were for the job, I explained that I did mission work and was good with people. I admit that it wasn't a great response. Helping people in mission activities translated into helping and serving people in sales. At least I thought so. She didn't see things my way at all.

Her thoughts were that salespeople had to be tough and be able to get in the dirt when necessary. Being tough also meant that

I could deal with cursing around me without being offended. Someone that was tough would not be too timid to ask for the business. After the interview, I called to see where I stood. She brought up the "too nice" objection again. Predictably, I wasn't hired by that company.

Too nice. Wow. That person obviously thought I would never make it in sales in such a challenging industry. Maybe that put a chip on my shoulder. Here I am, twenty-plus years later, in the same industry, now consulting after having been a salesperson, sales manager, and VP of sales.

That interview was quite a contrast to one of my favorite sales books that I had read, The World's Greatest Salesman which has over four million copies in print! In it, one of the ten scrolls speaks of love as the motivating force in sales. I love people. I thought that I should be able to get a job in sales because of this fact. This was about the third or fourth interview where my background was not working in my favor. It was not as easy as I thought it would be to get an opportunity in sales.

Eventually, I found a company that saw my background as a positive. They believed I could be nice and succeed, thankfully. In fact, there are many of us that truly care and love people. We hear over and over again people who are in sales saying they are in sales because they are "people" people. "I like people." "I like to help people". I like to make people feel good. I enjoy solving problems. Why? Is it love for people? One may think so.

Who is the nicest person that you can think of? Many think of Jesus of Nazareth. This individual showed compassion on the lepers, the prostitutes, the tax collectors, criminals, and the downtrodden. Nobody would think that he was soft. He showed us there is no end to the kindness that can be shown to others. Was he strong? Was he committed to the cause to the very end? I will let you be the judge.

Are you the type of person that will hold the door open for people? Do you let other drivers merge into your lane even if it means tapping your brakes? When you are entering a line in a store at the same time as another person, do you slow down to allow them to go first or speed up because you don't want to wait for one more person? When telling a story to someone and we get interrupted, do we say "can I finish please?" or do we breathe and smile and let them have the floor knowing we will eventually be able to finish the story either there or somewhere else? Being nice means being nice wherever we are, hidden or in plain sight.

SIDE BAR

I recall many years ago while stopped at an intersection, I laid on the horn signaling for the car in front of me to go, yelling, "WHAT ARE YOU WAITING FOR?" Do you know that as fate would have it, I followed that car for two miles up the road into our church parking lot? She was a young mom with 3 kids and I was learning about patience as a young man. I ran over to her and embarrassingly apologized for my stupidity. 40 years later, I still recall that thoughtless move. Can we be nasty on the road and nice in front of people and still be honest with who we really are?

If we show simple acts of kindness whether it be towards the receptionist, the "gatekeeper", the janitor, the stranger, we will feel better about ourselves and help others feel good as well. Ignoring people in an office as you walk by them because your role is supposedly superior, is not in harmony with being kind.

Unfortunately, some in sales have decided to take advantage of people. They are like wolves in sheep's clothing. They may look helpful and sincere but they are all about themselves and their commissions. They are not reading this book or any book about ethical behavior. We are not like them. We truly care and love people. This is why we do what we do. In the big picture, being kind is integral to our success in sales and in life.

Being Kind does not Mean Being a Pushover

I was in an office sitting across from a purchasing agent. This person was new to the company and seemed to be trying to impress his boss, a VP who was also in the room. He clearly had no patience for salespeople and very early on said that all salespeople are liars and will say anything to get a deal. I said I was sorry he felt that way but that was not the case with me. He said, "Yeah, that's what you all say."

I looked at his boss and said, "I think we're done here and I will see myself out." So I got up and left. This was a large opportunity by the way but not worth compromising character. No deal is worth compromising your character.

I was irritated on the drive after that meeting. It was a nice account but what was I to do? Getting insulted was not what I was going to take. So I was going to move on and forget about it. Then something odd happened. Within a few weeks, my phone rang. It was the VP that was in the office with the rude purchaser. He apologized and said the purchasing agent had parted ways with their company and would like me to come back in. After explaining why I left, I decided to give it a go and return. Long story short, they became my largest client. I could not have predicted that outcome based on the first meeting. People of character prefer to do business with similar people.

Nice or kind people do not finish last in sales. This is not to say that there are nice people who don't last in sales, but that can be for many reasons. Hopefully, such ones are finding the necessary tools that are available to help them to be successful like this book and many, many others that have been written over the years.

SIDE BAR

Beware of The Company With Whom You Are Interviewing

Are the company and service you sell for aligned with your values?

Be careful of the type of sales opportunity you take. There are plenty of scammers as we mentioned that are looking for people to sell their scams. Typically they offer tons of money potential and pay very little salary, if any at all. Be careful. These companies are all about minimizing risk. Some will hire anyone that breathes. Research, ask for references, try to speak with people in that company who aren't in sales. See what kind of culture there is. How long have people worked there? That's always a potential red flag if there is massive turn-over. Check the hiring boards and see the comments. What are the customer reviews like?

When you are interviewing, you need to view that interview in a way that shows you, they are the right fit for you. The last thing you want is to find out that it's a boiler room mentality, where lying is acceptable, screaming at underperformers is allowed and you have just invested months only to find this out. On top of that, you may have missed out on a better opportunity by accepting this one. Interview as if you are dating someone for the long term.

With Whom Would The Client Like To Work

Think about the client. Who would you rather work with? Someone who is pushy, tough, cocky, stubborn, boorish, or someone kind or nice? Periodically the cocky, pushy person will get their share of the business but don't worry about them. When given the opportunity, most people will choose people who treat them well.

When I was selling in Washington DC, I came across a certain person pretty frequently in accounts. That person seemed to be everywhere and knew a ton of people. I thought how difficult it would be to come off victorious when I was competing for the same prospect. But little by little we started winning a good share of the opportunities. Interesting to say the least. This person had longevity in the market, knew tons of people, and had a good product to sell and typically at a much lower price.

With one particular new client who had previously done business with this individual, I asked why they switched vendors to work with us? The client said that the other person was obnoxious. He would drop in unannounced and stick around trying to get an order signed by being pushy. The client said, "We like your style. You aren't pushy, you respect us when we are busy and you listen." Being respectful of others and listening to them, are traits of those that are nice, right?

Getting back to that hiring manager that did not hire me, that person came to work for the company where I was eventually hired, within a couple of years from the interview, not as a manager but as a salesperson. That conversation was interesting.

"Harry, do I know you from somewhere?"

"Yes, I actually interviewed with you and you said I was too nice to be in sales."

"Oh, that's right, now I remember you."

One has to laugh...

Within a few months, that person was terminated. Something about fraudulently signing a contract for a client was the reason they were let go. Their practice of being a pit bull towards others, ultimately was not successful, in the end.

SWD MASTER TIP

Stick to your values. Be kind. Be nice. Be strong. You will have long-lasting success.

CHAPTER 5

Begin With the End in Mind

"People with goals succeed because they know
where they're going." ~Earl Nightingale

Who doesn't calculate the cost before they do something of importance? Isn't this just a great question? We can apply it to just about any endeavor we take on. How many of us decided to go on a trip or a vacation without first calculating what it will cost?

If we were building a home, wouldn't we start with plans and understand what one can afford first? Back in the Dominican Republic, there were countless homes that were started and never finished. One could drive or walk down almost any street and see unfinished houses. complete shells of concrete block walls, some were foundations only, some had several walls up but no roof. It was extremely odd at first to see these but, eventually, we got used to the sight of them. Sometimes, you would see cows or stray dogs hanging out in these "houses". Apparently, some did not calculate the full cost and the project died out before getting finished.

When it comes to selling, are we calculating the cost so to speak? Do we understand what it will take to succeed? Do we know how many clients we will need to earn a living? Is that number reasonable to attain? The calculation will be a big part of your success because it will give you targets to pursue that are realistic and achievable.

Let's Do The Math

Maybe we don't like math. This math pertains to your income so, hopefully, it is a bit more interesting for you!

How much money do you want to earn? Start with that. I know, as much as possible, right? Let's come up with a real number. Maybe it's $100,000 a year for kicks. What is the average commission for your sales? Suppose the amount you come up with is $1,000. What is your salary if there is one? Let's say it's $40,000. (Create your own worksheet with your own numbers.) If the average commission is $1,000 and you want to make $100,000 then you would need sixty sales in a year. That is roughly five sales per month, one and a quarter per week.

Ex: 100,000.00 Target Subtract $40,000 salary = $60,000 Needed

Average commission is $1,000. $60,000 divided by $1,000 = 60.

60 Sales divided by 12 months =5 per month.

If the average sale will pay you $6000 like a commission for a sale of a house, then you would need to sell about seventeen houses per year. Then we can break that down to three every two months. Is that achievable? Are you starting to see how targets work?

Calculating What is Needed To Build

We need to determine how many opportunities we need to be in, in order to get to the desired number of closed deals. Remember that we will not win every deal. Perhaps you will win one out of every three deals, or one out of every four. Knowing this will help.

Next, ask how many appointments or meetings do we need in order to get us to the opportunities desired? Is it ten appointments per week? Is it five? Is it twenty? We need to know. If you are trying to hit a target, you will want to know where the target is. Imagine having a blindfold on and trying to shoot a basketball through a hoop. Without knowing where the target is, it will be virtually impossible to hit it.

Out of the ten meetings you conduct, can you add two to your pipeline of people who will make a decision in the next twelve months? What is the number for this that your sales leader is sharing with you?

The next step is to determine the amount of activity required to get to the desired number of appointments per week? How many emails? How many phone calls? How many network events will you attend?

Can we break it down into touches? A call is a touch. An email is a touch. A conversation at an event is a touch. A walk-in cold call at a business is a touch. What is a reasonable number of touches in the day that you can make to pursue the overall goal? Some might say the number is fifty. That could be something like twenty phone calls, twenty emails, and five DMs on LinkedIn and maybe five conversations at network or chamber events or walk-in cold calls. Do you get the idea?

Ultimately our week could look like this: 250 touches, leads to ten appointments. Those ten appointments/discussions lead to two people in the funnel. Then it might be one out of every ten in the funnel will buy something over the next thirty days.

The key is to track your numbers. The more you know about your actual numbers of calls and touches, the more beneficial it will be for you. This isn't to say that sales is just a numbers game. That implies that we could be robots and robotically do everything without working on our skills. Selling requires skills but the skills aren't going to matter if we are not in front of enough people.

Now let's determine your value per hour. Suppose you want to earn $100,000 per year. How many hours are you willing to work per week to get to that figure? Thirty? Forty? Fifty? Sixty? Eighty? For fun, let's say forty hours.

100,000.00 divided by 52 weeks = $1900 per week.

$1900 divided by 40 hours = $48 per hour.

(My first job paid me less than $3 per hour. What did your first job pay?)

Here is another thought, out of the forty hours per week, how many of those hours are truly productive? Sometimes we salespeople say we are working hard and yet many of us spend too much time doing busy work. Clearing out old emails and reading emails that have nothing to do with you or your business, shuffling papers around, driving to appointments when they could be done over a Zoom or virtual meeting, long lunches with co-workers, are all time wasters. You may find that out of the forty hours, that the time in front of people, sending emails, calling people, etc only adds up to about twenty hours per week. Imagine if we added a few more hours of productive time. Would that help with your income goals? I bet it would!

Once you are focused on the target and know your numbers, there is no doubt that you can finish what you started. I spoke to a business owner once who wanted to grow his business. I asked how many clients he had. He didn't know. I asked how many would he like to add to his business, he answered "more". That is a pretty elusive target. Once we clarified how valuable the number is, it allowed him to see the light and focus. The same can be true for us. The sooner we figure this out the better. The numbers will work. How many clients do you need? Whatever the number, knowing that number allows you to aim with clear vision at the target putting you in a better position to hit it!

SWD MASTER TIP

Take the time to learn your particular numbers. Whether it be the average sale, average commission, number of clients needed, the number of people to meet each week, all of these will help us to have specific targets that we can aim for. Our business will grow much faster if we do!

CHAPTER 6

Build on a Solid Foundation

*"Build your empire on the firm foundation
of the fundamentals." ~Lou Holtz*

We live in a world where we want results today. Who of us thought we could lose weight by taking a miracle pill and within a few weeks could shed twenty pounds and keep it off? We want instant gratification. If we want abs, we can buy something to give us abs. Some may not want to wait and decide to go to the surgeon to get their body "sculpted" almost instantaneously. Whether it be fast food, immediate access, delivered groceries, 5G, we want it now, if not sooner.

Sales leaders and business owners want results immediately. The system typically expects results inside of ninety days and many get cut from the team if they aren't producing. Bad month, okay but not two in a row! Some companies have the practice of hiring and firing sales teams every year, if not sooner! There is not enough time in ninety days to lay a foundation. One needs to view it like crops where we plant, fertilize, water, nurture, and eventually harvest.

In the world of selling, how does one build a solid foundation? I have had sales reps decide that no one is buying in their territory.

They hit every business and could not find a single buyer in the first 90 days and felt like it just wasn't going to work out where they could succeed. At the end of 90 days, they still didn't know anyone. They did not have any relationships. They went after the quick sale and did not start with building some kind of foundation.

They say things like: "The problem is my territory. If I had a better territory, I would be selling." Some in the larger cities will say it's too competitive in the city. Whereas the person in the smaller cities and towns complains there isn't as much opportunity as there is in the larger cities. The grass is always greener on the other side if that's the way You choose to look at it.

Are you familiar with the Acres of Diamonds story? This story was related by Russel Conwell back in the 1800s over 6,000 times. Yes, he went viral so to speak with the popularity of his speech! In it, he explains how there was a man who was quite content with his life. However, he was told about the riches related to diamonds. The man became obsessed with finding diamonds so he too could have those riches. He sold his home and land and traveled all over looking for diamonds. He eventually lost his money and due to despair threw himself into the sea. (apparently, he was a poor swimmer and it didn't end well.)

Naturally, the person that bought the land from the farmer and poor swimmer, saw what looked to be a diamond in a stream. Upon further investigation, it was indeed a diamond. In fact, with a little digging more diamonds were uncovered until eventually there were acres of diamonds found. The farmer had the diamonds right under his nose the whole time. Instead of digging and looking for the diamonds nearby, he went to look elsewhere for them, never to find them.

If we don't think diamonds are nearby, we won't be looking for them and we surely won't find them. Instead of complaining and looking at greener pastures, wouldn't it be better to work in the field we have? If we do, there is a high likelihood of finding the "diamonds". As a sales leader, I often would see delivery trucks from our competitors, delivering new technology in territories where "nobody was buying" according to the salesperson. Obviously, *somebody* was buying!

A great example has to do with an employer for whom I have mad respect, named Robbie Siemon. He has been the owner of Halsey and Griffith/HGi Technologies for decades. In fact, the company will be 100 years old in 2021. Part of the reason for the company's success is due to Robbie being involved with the Kiwanis Club in his hometown and other organizations. From the relationships built in that community, many have become clients for life. Even as he has approached the age where some consider retiring, Robbie took on the responsibility of joining a new networking group as a member to continue growing his relationships and in turn growing the business. This has resulted in some significant new diamonds getting discovered in a very short time. By the way, Robbie is probably one of the quietest people I know. Yet he is conversational and cares about people, *and treats everyone with dignity too*, which shines through his quiet demeanor.

How much better it would be to start building up relationships instead of randomly looking for opportunities without building relationships? Are we networking with people? Are we finding potential clients on LinkedIn and local business journals? How are those businesses faring? If they are doing well, one would ask if they could be a candidate for our services? How many businesses are potential candidates in our assigned area? Is there enough to earn a living if we put in the required effort?

Imagine starting conversations with just two people a day. After the conversation, we send a nice thank you email and mention how we look forward to the next conversation in a few weeks or months depending on the situation. Well after ninety days, based on the math of two per day, that is 180 conversations. Now, what if it was three per day? Four? You get the idea. That foundation can be built very solidly if we do things the right way early on. It will take some time, but it will produce the diamonds.

SWD MASTER TIP

We should not be overly concerned about the territory or region we are in. If other businesses are thriving, ours can as well. Let's look for potential clients in our area and work the long game. You can become well known in your area by many and be the "go-to person" when they need the services you provide. Lay the foundation solidly, build relationships that will be as valuable as diamonds. They will pay off just as they did for the farmer who "discovered" the diamonds right under his nose.

Section 2
Tactical Applications, Strategies and Stuff That Really Works

CHAPTER 7

Let's Get It Done (Git Er Done)

"Don't be an extra in your own movie. Move out of your comfort zone. Don't be afraid of feeling uncomfortable or awkward. Step out and make it happen." ~Bob Proctor

You Are the CEO of Your Business

Larry the Cable Guy has one of my favorite catch phrases of all time. Git-R-Done. I liked it so much I put it on my car license plate. Why did I choose that? It was like the phrase "Just do it" from Nike. When was the last time you really wanted something and found a way to achieve it? When you accomplished whatever it was, you no doubt sensed a feeling of pride. Sure there may have been some help along the way but if you didn't take the initiative, you would not have done it. Whether that be climbing a mountain, getting a degree, starting a new job, or whatever the desire may have been. If you really wanted it and decided not to pursue it, there is no blame. You just made the decision *not* to pursue it. Simple.

If you are in sales, it should not be viewed as a job. We show up to a job. Sales require much more than showing up. It's just as if you are running your own business. If you already own your business, this may be of value too. As the owner of your territory, what is the value of the opportunity that is in front of you? Some salespeople earn well above six figures when they develop the skills and have the work ethic. Some can even earn high six figures or even seven figures annually. Not all CEOs earn this type of income.

Now just as a person starting a business or buying a franchise may have dreams of earning a high income, they have to work in harmony with the dream. It doesn't just come to them. A person who enters the world of sales may be around people who are making significant incomes but that doesn't transfer over to the new person. Each has to create their own "empire" so to speak. It is as Larry The Cable guy would say "Git-R-Done!" It ultimately depends on *us* to make things happen.

Keep Knocking

This is where the knocking on opportunity's door comes in. We can want and wish for Opportunity to knock on *our door*, but it doesn't work that way. We need to do all of the knocking proactively. As the owner of our own destiny, we are ultimately responsible for everything that is tied to our success or failure. We can't rely on others to knock on the door, it has to be us. We are the best ones for the job since we have the most passion to earn our own income. Nobody wants to earn *your* income as you do!

Have you ever asked someone how business is and they respond with it's so-so or okay or slow? What are they doing about it? Are you envisioning them knocking on doors? If they were to knock on doors of opportunity would they be in the predicament? There are many business owners that fail simply because they wait for customers to walk into their store. Whether our store is brick and mortar or online, we cannot have the attitude of *wishing* people would walk into our "store".

I know of this sign store owner who is very successful and has had the store humming along for many years. What is his secret? He was proactively out and about every day meeting people in business. He was *outside* of his brick-and-mortar store speaking to businesses and building relationships. As people needed signage, who was top of mind? The funny thing is immediately after he signed documents to buy the franchise years ago, he found out that he was the third owner in three years! The previous two owners failed within a year! What does that tell us? It's not the location or the economy. It is all about us taking ownership of our destiny. By the way, this fellow had no sign store experience. It was a completely new venture. He didn't know signs but he knew how to have conversations with people.

Taking Ownership

As the owner of our destiny, we need to have or build habits that are conducive to success. Do we get up early or sleep in? Showing that we are industrious, taking ownership of every problem that arises and handling it immediately, without worrying about who's to blame is the mark of a winner. Some instead will look at a problem and point fingers, even saying it's not my job to solve that. If we use the word job, then that is a sign we are not "owning" our destiny. Now it's a given that others have jobs to do in the business but if they drop the ball, hopefully help where we can and not go down the blame road. As the owner, we have to take care of the client. Sometimes that means we need to reassure them. Taking ownership means we protect the reputation of the company and our employees or coworkers.

In the business I was in, there were many involved in the post-sale process. Orders need to be processed, equipment needed to be ordered, then set up, tested, delivered, and then installed at the client site. Typically six or seven people at least were involved in these steps after the sale was made. Any one of them could make a mistake that would affect the outcome of a smooth delivery and installation. When that mistake is occasionally made, do we blame or work as a team? I have heard people over the years do quite a bit of blaming to save face in front of the client by blaming the person in finance or on the delivery team by saying things like "I don't know why that happened, I told them..." What did that statement do for the client? Did they hear the salesperson undermine their own coworkers? Saving face should not be a concern. It is far better to say "I will get right on it!" when a problem arises than blame someone for the problem. Isn't that what the client wishes to hear? Owners take responsibility.

Taking Ownership Example

Curt, who has been selling with dignity for many years, is one who treats his clients like family and acts as the CEO of his own business. A company for which he was doing well with bringing on new clients was in effect bought out. Feeling concerned for one client in particular who made a substantial investment in Curt's product, he went back and told him about the change. He told the client that if he were to need anything or had any issues, he had Curt's personal contact information.

The client was stunned by this gesture and with a puzzled look on his face, sought clarification. "Then who is paying you to meet with me today?"

"No one," replied Curt. "You've placed your confidence in me as well as the products I represent. You should have confidence that I will do whatever I can to support you."

After a few silent moments to let that answer sink in, the client looked Curt straight in the eyes and said, "Well, whatever company hires you, tell them that you'll be bringing our business to them, as well."

Curt viewed his clients truly as *his*, as if he was the CEO of his company. They invested not only in his service but in him as well due to the trust he built up. With this type of ownership, people could recognize the type of support they were getting from him and this made him quite successful.

SWD MASTER TIP

We own our own destiny. There is no blaming others or making excuses. Opportunity does not come knocking. Creating our own opportunities is what we need to be doing every day. Our income depends solely on us. Everything we do will either cause us to succeed or fail. It is not the economy, the weather, the new president, the market, or whatever the flavor of the day excuse is. Bottom line, if we are not doing well then we need to look at the person in the mirror. We need to be honest with ourselves that we are not speaking to enough people that can potentially buy from us. Be like the third sign store owner and get out and speak to potential buyers of your services. The more we own our destiny, the better our chances are to succeed.

CHAPTER 8

Persistence Pays
(As Long As We Don't Give Up)

*"Many of life's failures are people who did not realize how close
they were to success when they gave up." ~Thomas Edison*

How much easier it would be if we only knew when the moment
of success would arrive. Is it just around the bend or is it down
the road for a way yet? It is like hiking up a mountain trail that
has an amazing view of a waterfall. After hiking for miles you
begin to feel the muscles in the body start to ache. Maybe the feet
are getting cramped or a blister is starting. You made it this far,
do you stop and start the descent? Or do you work through the
pain knowing that the reward is not that far away? Maybe a quick
rest is all you need but you fear that if you stop, it will be difficult
to start again. You have no real idea what the distance is left. Is
it another five minutes or another hour? It feels like it should be
close by.

You press forward. You made it this far after all. As you make
each turn in the trail, you see ahead another bend. When will
you get to the vista that shows the beautiful pristine waterfall?
Through the pain, you press on to make it to the last bend and
ahead you see a clearing. How do you feel now? The goal is now

in plain sight and you are only a few yards away. The energy picks up, the pain seems to dissipate as you climb the last few steps to see the amazing view. When you reach it, you are so impressed with what lies before you that you express your tremendous gratitude to the Creator for the beauty of the planet and for the fact that you continued to make the journey without quitting.

But what if you quit a few turns before the top? How disappointing it would be to find out we were only another few minutes from the reward. Some years ago, while my wife and I were in the Dominican Republic, we had just moved into a rural area and picked out what appeared to be a really beautiful house, in the daylight. The house sat on a hill with a magnificent view of rolling hills with tall palm trees and miles and miles of green grassy fields. What is different and something we really did not understand was the way windows worked. "Windows" in the Dominican Republic (and many of the islands) are slats of metal that crank open and close. There was not any glass in these windows nor were there screens. The roof was thatched with palm branches and spread across the top of the house but was not sealed from the top of the walls. This gap of a few inches allowed tropical critters to enter, which of course we did not really anticipate. We found *that gap was an issue* pretty quickly!

After we moved into the house that first day, we visited some new friends for dinner and stayed well after the sun went down. After we returned home, to that house high on the hill, we realized we were not alone in the house. We desperately searched for a light switch and found that we had *guests*. There were frogs, spiders, and cockroaches by the dozens. Incredibly, there were small birds flying around inside the house! What happened? It had been invaded!

We sheepishly went into the bedroom, thankfully we put up a nice lace mosquito net hanging from the ceiling that completely covered our bed. However, we saw the frogs and the flying roaches were trying to make their way inside of the net to join their roach friends who broke through the barrier somehow and were crawling around the bedspread and pillows! What we thought were small birds were actually palmetto bugs which are basically flying cockroaches that totally freaked us out. Can you imagine the thoughts going through our minds?

My wife looked at me with tears of disappointment in her eyes. If there was a hotel nearby and a plane back to the states, we probably would have jumped on the opportunity. But there wasn't anywhere to go. We had burned the ships, so to speak and there was no going back.

Within a few days, the bugs and frogs eventually moved out of our home with a little persuasion and some harsh bug sprays. After those first few days we only occasionally had to fight off a lizard or tarantula that would wander into our living space. The rest of our time there in that mountain area was full of amazing experiences with amazing people and beautiful scenery. We would have missed out on all of those experiences if we gave up and quit. It was like the hike where one was looking for that magnificent view that was just ahead. We made it to the top because we persisted. With gratitude, we enjoy amazing memories that we still reflect back on twenty-five years later!

Persist Until You Succeed

This is a nod to Og Mandino and his book *The Greatest Salesman in the World*. Pathros, a dying old wealthy salesman, gave the scrolls of secrets and principles to young Hafid. The third scroll was marked Persistence. I can't tell you how many times I muttered "I will persist until I succeed."

Selling is not easy and there are many reasons for this. We deal with rejection over and over again worse than what George Constanza on Seinfeld ever experienced. Whether we are waiting for the call from our own Vandalay Industries or looking at our email inbox for a single response from a prospect, we can't help but question if we are in the right business at times. It would be so much easier to get a regular job with a steady paycheck and give up on the dreams that selling can turn into reality.

In my case, I gave myself two years of being an apprentice in the new field of sales. Apprentices are learning a trade or a skill. Two years on the job and in the classroom will get a solid foundation. That will not make one an expert, just skilled enough to graduate into the job. With reading, coaching, practicing, role-playing, prospecting, following others, I was earning a living inside of two years. However, I was still not a pro yet. Selling, as I have mentioned, is all about people. So how long does it take to understand people and to be able to provide them with what they want and need, at times with only reading body language or understanding what isn't being said?

There are going to be days when you are frustrated. Weeks will go by where nothing appears to be positive. Months at times will look as though nobody is buying anything and occasionally a few months in a row will look very bleak. This is true with the economy in general and will, in all likelihood, happen with you. The key is to maintain your positive mindset despite the challenges. Keep doing the good work in times of challenge. If we keep planting and watering the seeds, the results will eventually come. We just don't know the day until that day arrives. It will come, only after we persist.

The farmer that is planting corn knows the plant will grow from the kernels that he plants and waters. He doesn't know exactly when the corn seedling will break through the soil. It depends on the warmth of the soil and other factors out of his control. He only can control a small piece of the operation. The same is true with you. You can't control when people will actually buy. However, you can control the amount of planting and watering you do with prospecting and nurturing.

A friend, who we will call Larry, is one who showed persistence. He was new to the business and had his share of early defeats. It was not looking promising for him. One defeat after another. After about a year of hard knocks, Larry was doing the right things and received a referral that seemed very interesting. It was a large company that was in the market for what he sells. They were unhappy with their current vendor and the main contact really seemed to like and trust him. The prospect after several meetings told him nothing was happening as the board was not ready to make a decision. Months went by. Larry got the call. The prospect said they were in the market for the end of the year. Larry jumped through hoops and provided what they asked for. The phone rang. It was the prospect. He said the board decided to hold off until the following year! Larry was disappointed and frustrated that all the work was for naught, to say the least.

The same prospect, a year later after he periodically spoke and met with the prospect and developed even better trust. Again as the end of the year approaches, Larry is told they are going to make a decision and to update the pricing. This is looking good, he was told. The information is all gathered. The prospect calls him with the news. They are holding off again! Larry, thick-skinned and all, was disappointed but still maintained his attitude of persistence. His manager was even implying to let this one go. He persisted.

More months passed. Finally, the prospect said we have the go-ahead, so update your proposal. Larry kept with it. He was still positive but kept his emotions in check as he had seen this movie before, so to say. What do you think happened? He got a call again and this time, the prospect shared the news. Larry was awarded the business! Larry won the business! There were songs of joy throughout the kingdom...oops I digress.

Larry persisted and eventually succeeded. For the sake of brevity, we left several other pieces out of this particular story where things looked very bleak. What happened next though was an example of how persistence truly pays. Not only did he get a very nice commission for his persistence, but his main contact also went to another large company, and guess who he called to come solve his problems at the new place? That's right. Larry got the call and the next deal was even larger than the first one.

Larry could have given up. It looked like he was being taken for a ride. However, he saw that the person was sincere and he stuck with him. Through all of the ups and downs, mostly downs, Larry *saw a positive outcome in the future.* He had no idea as to how long he would need to persist. He just kept persisting long enough to succeed.

Pass the Test

Buyers test salespeople all the time. Will they give up after one call? Two? Three? Or when they pop into the office and are told the contact is in a meeting, do they leave, never to return, or do they try again? The data shows that people need anywhere from five and fifteen attempts before they will have a conversation, let alone the idea of doing business with one.

One nice lady told me she would never take an appointment for at least a year of calling by a sales rep that she didn't know prior. Her line was "I'm busy you will have to call back". Most would stop after one attempt. Some would try two to three times. It was rare if anyone kept trying. The ones that did, would eventually be rewarded with a meeting. She wanted to see how patient and persistent the person was. Those are the type of people with whom she preferred to do business.

Do not tire of prospecting. A little bit every day will add volumes to your sales funnel. A friend of mine who is quite successful in his sales and coaching training business makes thirty calls a day like clockwork. He recently told me of one experience where a person decided to do business with him *after nine years* of calling. He reminded me that most salespeople do not make outbound calls. They wait for the business to come to them. One puts themselves in a much better position by seeking and knocking. Can you make thirty calls a day? twenty? Even ten is better than none.

As I am writing this book in 2021, my eighteen-year-old son told me he just set three appointments by making phone calls to new prospects. He was calling businesses on a Saturday! Who does that? People who want to succeed. They do things differently than the rest. I honestly did not think of making calls after hours until he just told me this. Interestingly, the day before we were having the conversation about prospecting and developing a sales pipeline takes time and to stay positive. Good things happen in time to those that put in the effort.

SWD MASTER TIP

Selling takes time from starting a relationship, finding pain with a prospect, showing there are solutions for the pain, and waiting for the prospect to actually commit to the solution as the answer to their problem and then committing to you. Remember that if there isn't a problem in their mind, they won't be buying. Even if they do recognize a problem, some sales cycles may take months to over a year from start to finish. Be persistent and do not give up. Success is right around the corner!

CHAPTER 9

Be Patient It's Not Only a Virtue, It Has Rewards

"Patience, persistence, and perspiration make an unbeatable combination for success." ~Napoleon Hill

"I wish they would hurry up and make a decision!" "We're not saving babies here! Just make a decision!" Have you ever shouted these words or something similar about a potential customer who keeps asking for more time or more information? I know I have!

That is just one example where we might lose our patience. Where does patience show up in sales?

A few areas where patience is required:

- Ghosting after someone tells us they are ready to buy
- When concerns arise
- The customer that complains about everything after the sale
- Patience for people that aren't buying according to *our* time frame

Ghosting After Someone Tells us They are Ready to Buy

This one probably will test our patience the most. "Why in the world would someone ask about the delivery timeframe, agreement to sign, and tell me they are ready to move forward and then just disappear?" I have either said this or heard others say this a hundred times over the years.

The key is to put ourselves in their shoes in every situation in order to relate and understand them better. Have we ever ghosted someone after we committed to buying something? I bet the answer is yes. Why would we do such a thing? We know we want the product or service. We know it will help us or solve a problem. Then these questions come up:

- Can it wait?
- Did we do all of the research we needed to do?
- Did someone raise doubt about the decision?
- Did something more urgent come up?
- Are we certain we won't have buyer's remorse afterward?
- Do we feel awkward about telling the salesperson because we committed but realized we weren't quite ready to do so?

These are some of the reasons people ghost us. They know we are there for them. They also know we aren't going away. When they are ready, they know we will be ready to help. What do they typically say to us after they reappear from being a ghost?

"I'm sorry this took so long, I appreciate your patience. Can we get this delivered tomorrow?"

So what can we do while being ghosted? The first step is pre-emptive. Try to avoid it in the first place. Always set up the next step with a specific time. When that occasionally fails, call and email with an empathetic tone. Liz Wendling, author of *Selling Without Selling Your Soul* suggests putting "yourself mentally into the last conversation and bring up what was said and how you are there to help them get what they need."

This works far better than laying the guilt trip or showing frustration. They will come around. Make it easy for them.

When Concerns Arise

Every buyer is different. They are looking at life out of their experiences, not ours. They may have been burned by previous salespeople. Perhaps they make decisions completely different from the way we do. Whatever the case, we cannot show frustration over the questions. Be helpful and understanding. Although they may raise objections repeatedly, they may not recall if they brought this up before with you or with some other salesperson. What may help is to send a recap email with their concerns that were already covered after a conversation.

Questions are important in moving the sale forward. If there aren't any raised along the way, the sale is probably not happening until something is raised. View that as a positive. You are moving closer to the sale.

The key is having empathy. Understanding the type of person they are will help us to relate to them better. We are not all alike. We may make decisions quickly but many are more methodical and need more data. Are we there to help them or do we move on because we are frustrated at their requests for more information or more time?

The Customer Who Complains About Everything After the Sale

First of all, let's hope that this one was worth the energy and effort. Some of the smallest customers make the most noise and need the most attention. The preemptive action is to pick up the traits of the complainer early on and decide if this relationship is going to be worth it. I have mistakenly viewed some of these types as a challenge and I could win them over in time. That rarely happens. There are just unhappy people in life and no matter what we do, we may never satisfy them.

Sometimes people hide the complaining attribute pretty well until post-sale. What is their fear? They may have buyer's remorse. They may fear the idea of making a mistake. They may fear that if something goes wrong they will be stuck.

Have you ever felt this way before? Immediately after you buy something and it isn't up to your expectations, do you complain? I know I do. What is it that you want to hear? We all want reassurance. We don't want to feel we are stuck with what we just bought. For these people, be reassuring. Saying things like "I am here for you" and "we aren't going anywhere" can put them at ease. In a little while, after things run smoothly a bit, they will be comfortable that their decision to work with you was a good one.

Patience For The One That Is NOT Buying On OUR Schedule

The end of the month is approaching. The sale we are counting on is slipping away. Our contact tells us that the signer had to leave for some emergency. The deal that would have brought you to quota just fell through. Do you let your emotions show? Or do you keep your dignity? Always being the true professional, you ask if everything is alright with the signer and her family. You are there for them. You know that patience is required in sales and in serving others. Good things come to those that wait as you know. It isn't easy but then again, anything that is worth it is not easy. Your patience will pay off.

SWD MASTER TIP

There are many areas where patience is a virtue in sales. Putting ourselves in the shoes of others will help us to maintain our good attitude and keep us from saying something we would regret. People are not trying to frustrate us personally. There are reasons they are delaying or are continually raising concerns. It is our job to get to the root of the challenges and help them to feel confident in working with us. When we do this, we will be showing that our patience definitely pays.

CHAPTER 10

Don't Waste Your Time...
it Eventually Runs Out

"Time is more valuable than money. You can get more money, but you cannot get more time." ~Jim Rohn

Many of us early on in sales love it when people show any interest at all. The key with people "showing interest" is to find out if they are a viable prospect for your services. Sometimes people are just nice and take meetings with any sales rep that calls them. It appears that this type of person needs friends. It was a running joke that the people that had the most interest had the least amount of money. I can't begin to describe the amount of wasted time I experienced by listening to people who expressed interest but there was no way they could afford what I was selling. If one is selling yachts, they best be calling on people who can afford a yacht. It really is that simple.

Not Everyone is a Candidate for Your Services

Being patient does not mean helping non-prospects to become prospects. Let them do that on their own. Trying to convince someone that they have a problem, is a misuse of patience when it comes to sales acumen. The time it will take to help convince someone they have a problem, is time that you can spend finding people that really do have a problem that you can fix. There are more than enough people who recognize they have a problem and have the money to do something about it.

People Who Want to See Every Imaginable Option or Scenario

There will be those that ask for pricing on everything. They have nothing better to do with your time than to waste yours it appears. Don't fall into the trap. Its paralysis by analysis. This overthinking is paralyzing the decision-making process. These are the same type of people that would look at a gigantic menu and ask the server what each item is. The server does not have that kind of time. They would ask possibly what the guest was in the mood for. With that response, they could narrow down some options. Some people need to have fewer options to make a decision. They may ask for many, but with practice, you will be able to say something like, based on what you have heard so far, which of these seems to be more realistic for your particular need. Narrow down the options for your prospect. You have the skills. If they still don't budge, it is best to move on. They aren't buying anytime soon, if ever.

Spend More With The Spenders

Not every client has the same value. Some will spend much more than others. The frequent fliers for the airlines get better discounts and more perks because they spend more than the average passenger. The airlines treat people who spend more, better than the ones who spend little. It's a fact. It isn't that they treat the infrequent flyer poorly, they treat them well enough. But the big spenders get even better service.

With this comparison, are you spending your time with your clients that spend more? The larger accounts typically can buy more from us than smaller ones. The relationship-building should be done more with ones who are going to help your business more. Don't feel bad about that. When you are off the clock and want to spend time with a client who is nice but buys very little from you, it's okay to meet for an occasional coffee. You may find nice people in larger accounts too though.

Selling time Versus Non-selling Time

There are activities that require our attention that can be done after hours and definitely not during peak selling time. An example of this is researching companies to find good prospects worth calling. Many years ago I worked with a person who was doing very well in sales. One of his tricks was to have his laptop in front of him during his weekend watching sports; it gave him time to research the accounts he planned to prospect during the week. Compare that idea to the salesperson who between phone calls to prospects spends time researching. So the one who is prepared ahead of the call time can get twenty to thirty calls or more in an hour where the researching caller combo person is getting about five to six calls in an hour. Big difference in productivity. Who do you think would have a better chance for success if skills were comparable?

Windshield Time

If you are in business to business sales, you want to be smart about your drive time between calls. Try to schedule appointments near each other instead of driving all over the map. You will be far more productive by doing so. Driving is not selling. If you can get some meetings as a virtual meeting that will save you the drive time. Years ago I watched my friend Dennis map out his day of appointments with red pins that he would stick on a map that hung on his wall. Today we have apps for this but driving to appointments in some kind of order will save us time and gas money too! Depending on traffic, a one hour appointment may take two hours or more with drive time. It might make sense to put a dollar value on the appointment. If the client is not a decent percentage of your monthly revenue, maybe you just do virtual meetings with them. Save the in-person meetings for those that are spending more with you, if this makes sense to do based on your particular business.

SIDE BAR

Give yourself time to arrive early. You can be 15 minutes early and get some last minute stuff done while you are sitting in a lobby waiting for the client meeting. It is so much better mentally to be early and people will view you as a true pro. Besides, your client will view you as a time waster if you are showing up late to their meetings. There are some people who will not do business with people who show up late. It's easy to be on time with just having the mindset that you will always be early.

Emails and the Calendar

Email can be one of your biggest time wasters. Some salespeople boast about how clean their inbox is. If you are spending time during selling hours cleaning out your email, it is not a good use of time. If we recognize the email is spam or some other time-waster, don't open it. If you do, move to Spam or Unsubscribe. Best to do those while watching Netflix though.

Another challenge for some is responding immediately when they get an email. You are not under obligation to do this. You can set the time that you will check emails and if someone asks something from you, offer to have an answer by the end of the day. A good practice would allow you to open emails and respond every couple of hours. Pet peeves, sending an email to say you will get the answer and then a second email with the answer five minutes after the first email. Does the person who sent the email want to get an email in return stating you will get an answer or are they happy to wait for the answer and actually get just one email instead of two? Another pet peeve is CC'ing people that really do not need to be part of the conversation. Now we can be wasting others' time too. Think of it this way, you are speaking to someone in the office. Do you need to get someone else in the conversation too? If not, then no need to CC someone in the email.

The calendar is another great tool. If you absolutely need to get something done, block off the time on the calendar to do it. If you see it in your calendar, you are more likely to get it done. I have had many To-Do lists but when I absolutely need to do something, it goes into the calendar. If you want something to get done, block off the time for it in your calendar.

SWD MASTER TIP

Be your best during peak selling time which usually means business hours. For some, it may be evenings and weekends. During the selling time, focus on selling activities like prospecting, meetings, or being with your clients. Save the other activities for non-selling time.

CHAPTER 11

We Have Two Ears and
One Mouth for a Reason

"Attentive listening to others lets them know that you love them and builds trust, the foundation of a loving relationship." ~Brian Tracy

Listening skills may very well be the most important of all of the skills related to the success of salespeople. Being great at listening is far better than being great at speaking when it comes to helping and serving.

Dale Carnegie in his timeless bestseller from the 1930s wrote a chapter on this topic. He said, "In order to be interesting, be *interested.* "People are a hundred times *more interested in themselves and their problems than they are about you and your problems.*"

Think of the salespeople you know. Are they good conversationalists or do they just like to talk? I have a friend, Barry, who was like a machine in telling people what they could get from his company. Talk about showing up and throwing up! He mistakenly believed if they ever did need something, they would remember something he said. The problem with that is people only *remember that one is interested in themselves and what they sell, not in serving their clients.* It took some time but Barry eventually started asking better questions and cut way back on telling the prospect everything the company did. His conversations improved and so did his sales.

A **good conversationalist** is one who can build rapport with the other person and get them to open up by *actually showing interest in them*. The key is asking open-ended questions instead of questions that only get a Yes or No response. Forget about "the pitch". Nobody, I mean NOBODY wants to hear these sales pitches anymore. We get bored with self-centered talkers and those who think selling is talking. It's as if we are vomiting empty, meaningless gibberish all over our prospect.

The Rule: Don't Interrupt!

We are speaking to a prospect, we ask a question about their business. They begin to speak, and start to tell us something valuable. However, because we can relate to what they are sharing, we interrupt just as they pause. Then they stop with their conversation. Why?

When someone is speaking they have the floor. We just can't interrupt. If this isn't a rule for true sales professionals, let's make it one!

"I had such good rapport, I could finish their sentences at times." News Flash! Not everyone wants you to finish their sentences! Sometimes a person may be more thoughtful in their speech or it just may take them a few seconds longer to translate thoughts into words. Be empathetic, patient, and kind. Finishing their statement may cause them considerable frustration although you thought you were being helpful.

What if the silence seems to be uncomfortable after you ask a question? How long do you wait for the person to respond? Anthony Iannarino says, in his book *The Only Sales Guide You'll Ever Need*, you should count to four after you ask a question. Try doing this. Practice it, he says. Eventually, get to five or six in your count. It allows people to finish their thoughts.

> ## SIDE BAR
>
> Be intentional with your listening. Our phone is a huge distraction and some text notification from a spammer can make us act like an addict. This appointment can be worth thousands or tens of thousands over time. Don't be the dumdum that needs to check their phone like they're waiting for a call from the White House. We should shut it off and put it out of our sight.

Understand what is being said

When people speak, do we always understand? Nope. Yet we don't ask for clarification. Why? Usually, because we don't want to look stupid. A simple way to do this is by saying: would you mind clarifying that for me? Or what does that mean for you?

Before we leave a topic, how can we be sure we understand? As your prospect is speaking you are jotting down some notes, keywords, or phrases, not entire sentences. To show that you understand, ask if we can summarize what they said to make sure we have the main points clear. Then restate what they said was important to them and ask "Did I get everything?"

It can go like this: *"Mary, thank you for sharing some of your challenges related to your environment. Just to be sure I have it all, would you allow me to summarize to make sure I didn't miss anything? First, you said that you are having a difficult time keeping staff in spite of efforts to be competitive with pay. Next, there are concerns about being competitive in the market due to consolidation. And the third item you mentioned, I could use a little clarification on...could you help me with that so I have it clear in my mind?"*

Is that painful? It's far better to leave with a clear understanding of their concerns than to walk away unsure. Far better to ask for clarification than to potentially miss an important issue.

Listen With Empathy

When we ask open-ended questions, we need to show that we care. If we rattle off one question after another, like a checklist, no one is going to think we care about them. It is better to ask a few questions and show empathy with the responses and build rapport than ask a ton of questions without empathy. Your prospect will begin to lose interest quickly.

Failure to Show Empathy

Early in my career as a sales manager, I was asked to visit an account with one of the team. I was told the client wasn't happy with us and I was confident we would help them and mend the relationship.

During the meeting, the client related several challenges. As they explained each one, I confidently said that we would fix it.

I apparently wanted to be Mr. Fix It. That was my ego talking. As much as I thought my confidence in solving each issue was a good thing, I clearly was not showing empathy. Upon leaving the meeting, I felt confident that things were good and we fixed the problem. Silly me.

Later I learned the client signed a nice deal with the competition. My associate told me the client thought I was cocky and insensitive. Wow, that one stung for a couple of reasons. One, it was a significant sale that we lost. Second, my pride was put in its place. I first reacted by blaming the ex-client for using me as his excuse to go elsewhere, but then I looked inward. My responses were such that I heard these issues all before and nothing was new here. I fixed other issues, I could fix these. I was like a doctor with no bedside manner.

From that day on, whenever someone is unhappy, they have the floor and I aim to be completely focused with good eye contact. Problems may be common but they are unique to each person who has them. Showing empathy means we recognize this fact. No matter how common the problem, people want us to show we understand them as unique individuals. Lesson learned.

Our goal should always be to understand others when they speak and even when they are silent. Being empathetic and caring will go a long way in building trust in our relationships, professional and personal for that matter.

SWD MASTER TIP

We should be asking good open-ended questions to our clients and prospects. But then more importantly we need to listen quietly to their responses. Listening, being present in the moment, while another is speaking, is a skill. It requires effort to improve. What is important is to show we are understanding, empathetic, and are truly listening. Once we do, the trust factor is established and people will share what they truly are feeling. Once that trust is established, they will tell us what we need to know in order to provide our solution to their problem.

CHAPTER 12

Win Big With a Little Humor

"If you can make 'em laugh, you can make 'em buy!"
~Old adage often shared by Jeffrey Gitomer

Back in the DR, the culture there was quite different when it came to the ways young men treated women. Guys would see my wife in a grocery store, on the street, in a bus, wherever and make catcalls, whistle, and make some kind of remarks that I did not understand based on the language difference. She was frustrated and I wanted to yell at them and tell them to shut up and get a life. Of course, my knowledge of Spanish was limited to about thirteen words and that prevented me from saying much.

One day, I'd had enough. After a long ride on the motorcycle out on dirt roads, we came across a little village. There in front of us was a little market with several young men drinking beer and hanging around the storefront. As we got off the motorcycle, the catcalling and whistling began. I took my helmet and hurled it to the ground and watched it bounce away on the gravel and then yelled "She is my wife!" in Spanish. This is the great part, *I either said I love myself* or *I love her,* or *she loves me!* All three of which are not very threatening and I knew as I said it that it sounded pretty silly! Hey, my Spanish was not the best! Of course, all the guys chuckled as they watched me spout off and probably wondered what I was trying to say. I think they got the point. I'm sure they have long forgotten the experience but we still laugh about it.

I have always enjoyed a good laugh. How about you? Kidding around with friends or family is just the way I prefer to be. In sales, you can have some laughs with prospects and clients. It *is* allowed. In fact, people may like you more if you are yourself and lighten up a bit!

With one particular new prospect while on the phone, I could tell that he was not really fond of salespeople. He was saying things like we are all alike and only cared about the sale and not about the client. In return, I jokingly said something that I thought was pretty funny about buyers being liars. Then there was SILENCE on the other end and after a few very long seconds, I heard a "what did you say?" *Uh-oh.* Time to back peddle and rewind what I just said. As I replied, stating that I was kidding, I heard a little smile in his voice and realized he was doing his best to make me squirm. It worked!

After that first conversation, we became even friendlier and on the way to becoming friends. I apologized a few hundred times! He ended up buying from me but definitely had to keep my pricing in line with competitive quotes. This went on for a few years. The trust was building. We had our share of laughs. He would buy and keep me honest with competitive quotes. It was pretty consistent.

Due to our growing friendship, I was invited to "The Christmas Eve Card Game" where a bunch of the managers and a select few vendor partners would spend a few hours playing cards, eating unhealthy foods, possibly enjoying an adult beverage, and would have tons of laughs. The story of how I was made to squirm on that first call and the way he told it, was priceless. I would always let them pick on me and I would laugh along with them at my expense. After that first card game, this new friend of mine ended up buying a considerable amount with our company, and that practice of comparing the price I offered with competitors, went bye-bye. The trust factor was high and it all started years earlier with that first conversation laced with a bit of humor!

However, when I was new to sales prior to this, I was tense and nervous and *so* serious too. I didn't realize that business could be fun and one could truly bring humor and laughter into the business or sales environment. The anxiety of learning what was new, selling to businesses, learning about my product and the various applications for it, and the software that was important to users, all of that was pretty serious for me. So, naturally, with the serious mindset and trying to sound fairly intelligent when speaking the new language with technology, it was fairly nerve-wracking and because of that, I was in serious mode.

In time as things started to settle and I became more comfortable with everything, I also realized that some people were having a lot of fun in their businesses. Although I was told to be "myself" on numerous occasions by my manager it took a while to figure that out. Eventually, I adopted that mindset to have fun selling whenever and wherever I could. Even in fairly serious situations, I would look for ways to break the ice. An example might be when reviewing a proposal and finding typos. Yes, I say that in plural because many who are in sales are not detailed individuals. So as much as we may review something, inevitably we will find a mistake here and there, and typically it was with numbers. Instead of breaking out into a cold sweat and freezing up at a glaring error, I would say in front of the client something like "oopsie that's not right. My bad" Cross it off with a pen and handwrite what was accurate. Oopsie is not a technical term but it comes in handy when a mistake is made and you want to make light of it a bit.

Another way of using humor is self-deprecation. For people like me who are bald to say something like I am having a bad hair day if it's windy or rainy. Most people with hair can relate to bad hair days but it becomes funnier when bald people use the expression. It definitely is a good way to break the ice when meeting some people in a conference room. Expressions like:

I'm just a little slow today

"Still learning English when" you get tongue-tied or find a typo

I must not have had enough coffee

or my dog ate some of the notes I took

I'm late "due to traffic" even for a Zoom meeting

Typically these types of comments will get a smile and break the tension and build trust that you are a regular person.

Silly, harmless humor. It seems to warm up people. Self-deprecation works well when you are highlighting a minor flaw. For instance, many will poke fun at their weight, in my case I mention my flowing locks of hair getting messed up on a windy day and similar comments. According to Dr. Marty Nemko, who wrote The Case for Self Deprecation in Psychology Today, states, "Self-deprecation can be used to diffuse antipathy, express humility, lower expectations to a reasonable level, and reduce excessive self-confidence. 'It prevents you from appearing holier-than-thou.' Since many view salespeople as somewhat self-centered and overly confident, this tool can disarm people and have an endearing effect."

In today's world where people may get offended over just about anything, it still is difficult to be offended at poking fun at oneself when done tactfully over minor flaws. However, poking a little fun at the client is *not* a good idea. No matter how light-hearted some may appear, we just don't know the type of day a person is having. Even with my own family or coworkers, I could get a "not in the mood for it" comment from someone. So once we hear that, it's best to let it go and realize the person is going through something. Empathy is required in that case.

One of the best times to use a little humor is when doing any kind of post-sale training on your product. People are generally in a good mood. They are excited about the new product and if you bring some life and fun into the training with a little humor and maybe a box of cookies, you will create a nice experience for the client and they will see you as being much different than many of the cold, boring training that were provided by so many others.

Even if you may not have a funny bone in you, it doesn't mean that you can't have some fun with your client. I know a nice woman in sales we will call Michelle who is very friendly and outgoing. She is frequently taking clients out for lunch or bringing lunch to her clients to sit with them and small talk. She will tell me "you know, she and I are friends" regarding many of her clients. If you were to see her in action, self-deprecation comes out frequently whether it be a comment about her "hundreds" of pairs of shoes or purses or her jabs about needing to lose weight, all of this builds up the friendship and trust factor. People would rather do business with someone who is fun and a regular person.

Humor and just being your friendly self can be instrumental in building friendships, breaking down barriers, and making people feel comfortable. In business and in sales, there indeed is a time for humor!

SWD MASTER TIP

Humor puts people at ease. Given a choice, most people would rather work with someone who is providing an enjoyable experience. Think of the car insurance commercials. Years ago they were stale and boring. Then Geico changed it up. Progressive, Allstate, Liberty Mutual, Farmers, all followed suit. Humor was the key to help people remember them when they need car insurance. Similarly, show the lighter side of you with your prospects and clients. You may be surprised to learn that people will like the fun you, more than the serious you. Are you having some laughs with your clients? Walt Disney said, "If you can laugh together, you can work together." Go ahead, laugh a little!

CHAPTER 13

Humility Rises to the Top

*"Practice radical humility when it comes to your
own accomplishments, and give credit everywhere
except to your ego." ~Wayne Dyer*

While living in the DR, we were learning to speak Spanish. Reading Spanish with a dictionary is a lot different than speaking and listening in Spanish. If you ever had to speak another language in a foreign country, you know what this is like. It is humbling. Imagine that a three-year old has a better grasp of the language than you do.

When we were brand new to the island, we got on a bus to go into a mountain town to meet some new friends. The road to this mountain town, Constanza, was one of those roads that were cut into the side of a mountain. One would be lost forever if their vehicle drifted off the road and fell into the canyon below. Guardrails? No, those were not a thing back then, in the 90s anyway.

The bus was full of Dominicans with loud Bachata and Salsa music playing. Of course, we did not speak Spanish and understood even less. Maybe combined, we could speak about twenty words in total. *Dinero, jugo, Americanos, cerveza* and a few others! The bus ride was fascinating with amazing views. However, I was dreading the thought as to where we would get dropped off once we reached the town. There were no cell phones and no internet back then. I was thinking that maybe the bus dropped everyone off in a town square and there we would meet our friends. No such luck. The bus actually had a route and people got off at various stops. Finally, the bus was emptied and my wife and I were left to ourselves with a very limited vocabulary. Two *Americanos*, it was late and getting dark and we had no idea where we needed to be.

The town was far bigger than anticipated. So we threw out the word *iglesia*, this means church. The bus driver probably asked which church or something similar but we didn't understand anything he said. Patiently he drove us around the town looking for churches. Eventually, we found what we were looking for, thanks to the kind and helpful bus driver who took pity on us! That was just one of the dozens of occasions where we had to depend on the kindness of strangers. You know what, people were very understanding of our lack of *understanding*!

These were lessons in humility for me. Thankfully my wife picked up the language faster than I did so if we were together, we did pretty well. Alone, I was hoping I could walk into a store without having to speak to anybody, and God forbid, no one asked me a question because my only response was "I don't know!"

I don't know is not something to be ashamed about

How does this translate (pun intended) into sales? Just as I had to get comfortable with "I don't know", sometimes we need to make similar statements in sales. Occasionally the prospect will use terms that we are not familiar with. Or they may ask us something that we may not know the answer to. Do you mind telling a prospect that you do not have all of the answers? Or does the idea of saying "I don't know" make us cringe?

I have watched some salespeople try to bluff their way through an answer that makes them look foolish. Once we go down that path of bluffing, be prepared to taste shoe leather, because your foot will end up in your mouth. That taste is not great by the way.

If you are selling something that may be a bit complex, you probably don't know everything there is to know about your product. It's okay. In fact, with more complex products and solutions, one may have a specialist involved to answer the more technical questions. Even they at times will need to find an answer that eludes them occasionally.

Many times, I have met prospects that know more about what I was selling than I knew myself. They were quick to test my knowledge. The humble person is smart to *avoid pretending* that we know more than they do. So why not let them know early that you still have plenty to learn.

Think about it, the person selling computers is not going to know as much as the person who is programming computers. The sales representative selling surgery tools to the surgeon is not going to know as much as the surgeon. People that use what we sell day in and day out may just know more than we do.

You can win these people over quickly by deferring to them. Let them win the product knowledge contest. They will feel good about themselves and will respect you more for doing so. You are not being "shown up" because they know more than we do.

One of many lessons in humility for me was given by a client while I was training a group on a print system that was quite expensive in a graphics company. I really should have had a specialist with me but I wanted to get better and sometimes the best way to learn to swim is to jump right in the water so to speak.

This particular client used the technology I provided eight hours a day for years and knew it like the back of their hand. I was showing some of the fundamentals and quickly learned I was not in their league. As I turned away for a few seconds, one of the groups played a trick on me and made an LCD screen go dark. As I turned back and saw the blank screen, I started panicking and pressing buttons and mumbling softly things like:

"There must be some glitch..."

"I have never seen this..."

"I need to call support..."

After a minute of what seemed like an eternity, the leader of the group was asking if it was broken already? Seeing my desperate look he laughed heartily and reached over and moved a hidden dial that brought the LCD screen back to life.

Did I feel stupid? You betcha! Yes, I was humbled a bit, to say the least! But I laughed nonetheless, it was pretty funny after all.

Not everyone would react the same way. Some would have gotten angry with the prankster and that could have worked out completely differently. When we are shown that we may not have the answers, pride is only going to make it worse. The shared laughter actually strengthened the relationship. I was one of them, part of the crew so to speak. They pranked each other regularly so I felt honored once I knew that. That story stuck with us for years as they continued to buy regularly from me and we all eventually became card-playing pals.

Frequently, it's how we project ourselves when we are asked a difficult question. Get comfortable with this phrase: "Great question! I don't have the answer for you at the moment, but I will get it for you." Then get the answer as soon as you can and get back to them as promised!

SWD MASTER TIP

It is perfectly fine to tell or show your prospective client that you do not have all the answers. What will that mean for them as far as trust is concerned? Do you think trust will grow or shrink because you do not want to give the wrong answer? They can expect that when they ask you a question, that you will do your best to find an accurate answer. You will not be labeled as a slimy salesperson that would say Yes to anything in order to get a deal. People will understand that you do not know everything. Humility in sales goes a long way in building trust and relationships that truly last. You will rise above the others by showing you are humble.

CHAPTER 14

Choose Your Friends Wisely

"Surround yourself with only people who are
going to lift you higher." ~Oprah Winfrey

If we are hanging around people who are trying new things, living life to the fullest, working on improvement, or making the world just a little bit better, do we benefit by being with such ones? Of course!

Have you ever heard the phrase, "Iron sharpens iron"? That, too, came from the Good Book. Just as a knife can get dull over time and periodically needs to be sharpened, the same is true with us. What are we doing to sharpen ourselves? Just being alive is not sharpening the knife. As the knife gets used regularly, it will get dull over time. The longer we avoid getting sharpened, the duller we become. Look at the habits we have. How many of us binge-watch Netflix like this is worthy of a trophy? We spend hours daily on Facebook looking at the lives of others instead of living our own life to the fullest. Yet these same types of people when given an opportunity to improve, the first thing out of their mouth is either no time or no money. Seriously, are we to live our life without even trying to be the best version of ourselves? I certainly hope that if you are reading this, you will want to improve.

If you are spending your time with people who are underachievers, without vision, stuck in life, negative about growth, energy vampires, what kind of influence will that have on you? Instead of being being lifted higher, you would drop to their level. Not that we don't try to help those that want it but if they prefer to be where they are with no growth, it may be time to find new friends.

As you consider your friends and perhaps you are thinking they are not helping you in aiming for the stars. I am not suggesting that you should act like you are better than others and this is not about making judgments against people. But as you focus on improving yourself and making new friends, you will find that you will have less time for the unsupportive ones.

Where can you find these new friends? One place is on LinkedIn. There are many positive, bright, people of influence there. As you search for people and see business executives, authors, coaches, business owners, leaders, and others that may share your interests, start connecting with these winners. They will post articles and stories that will help you to develop.

You will be amazed at the types of people that you will meet over time. Again, this will not happen overnight but within a relatively short time, your circle of friends can be much different and much more impactful with positivity in your life.

How many of us think of reflecting daily on gratitude? What about having morning routines that help us get the day off to a great start? How many of us wish we would find more time to exercise, read, eat better, treat others better, have better relationships with our children and spouses? What about improving with our business acumen, sales activities, motivation, spirituality, and peace of mind? All of these topics are found with hundreds more about various types of businesses too. Facebook for many is entertainment and watching others live their lives while LinkedIn is for developing better relationships and improving our lives and helping others improve theirs.

Here are some changes I have made that were either influenced or encouraged by others on LinkedIn. Podcasting, speaking, writing a book and articles, creating video content, daily morning ritual, better conversations through connections made, better relationships, business ideas, mastermind groups, international friendships, and the list goes on. Sorry Netflix, Facebook, DirecTV, and other media, I have none of this from you.

Our knife sharpening can also take place with books and video. You are reading this book and hopefully, it is sharpening the knife. There are others that will do the same. Even authors who have long left this world, are still providing guidance for those of us who are looking for it. Napoleon Hill, Earl Nightingale, Og Mandino, Wayne Dyer, and Jim Rohn are a few that I either read their words, listen to on podcast channels or watch them speak on YouTube. The lessons are priceless and can help you change yourself for the better.

Others who are still going strong include Bob Proctor, Les Brown, Joyce Meyer to mention a few. Even if we don't like to read, there are books on audio, podcasts, YouTube, and I am sure there are other places as well. How simple is it to put these influencers on and have them play while we commute, exercise, have our morning coffee, or relax before we retire for the night? While many talk about news events that are divisive, depressing, or discouraging, we can share positive thoughts, ideas, and concepts with others and sharpen each other as we do.

As we look at the knife that has become dull, we now have all kinds of tools at our disposal to use to sharpen the knife. What will we do? Knowing the tools are there will not get the job done. Action is required. Where can we improve individually? Are we aware of the areas? Are we completely happy with our income, the way we look, the way we move around, the outlook for the future, our relationships with our family, our relationship with our Creator, and our view of ourselves? Many of us can work on all of these and we can without being overwhelmed. Little by little, we sharpen the knife. We read or listen to something from one of these knife sharpeners and ask "how can I apply this?" Then think for a few minutes and mull it over. Then, look for ways to put it to use. Try it immediately and start building the habit. Before long, you will be in a much better position than you were a week ago, a month ago, a year ago. It may look like a long road ahead, but looking back, you will see that you traveled quite some distance on the road to improvement.

SWD MASTER TIP

We should always be looking at ways to live and Be our best selves. It does not happen just by living. We need to surround ourselves with people who help us on this journey. People who are looking out for our best interests, not those who are content with the status quo and just to live life without giving it any real thought. What is your potential? You will be amazed if you open up your mind and start connecting with winners and associating with them. You will be sharpened in a way you may never have thought was possible. Where will the journey take you to your best self?

CHAPTER 15

Call Me Cliche...Teamwork
Really Does Make The Dream Work

"Great things in business are never done by one person.
They're done by a team of people." ~Steve Jobs

Some people will say things about salespeople like "Salespeople only care about themselves. They are self-centered, egotistical, brash talkers, generally they are people to avoid." That sentiment may be true in some cases but certainly not all. Those who are heart-centered or are driven by love for others, sellers with dignity, will stand out from the rest.

With a survival of the fittest culture, some companies like to pit sales people against each other. They say salespeople perform best due to the spirit of competition. But this type of competition is far from friendly. You can walk into these places and you will find there is a culture of distrust. No one wants to mention any names of prospects in fear another rep will steal that account away. The culture is dysfunctional. Yet, everywhere else in the company they expect the team to operate as a unit. On one hand, they say this and out of the same mouth they refer to the salespeople as a "team". What team would ever succeed if they all were against each other? A team of individuals in any sport will not get very far. They need to operate as a team, together on a mission.

If you are in a company like this, I suggest that you find another person with a similar mindset as you and build a team of two. Add others to the team as they start to see the value of working together. Before long, you can change the culture. Management will see what you are doing and it may change their thinking. They will look to you as examples. This does happen occasionally if the leadership has any character. If they don't, there are plenty of sales opportunities out there with companies that would welcome someone with dignity.

Go Alone Go Fast, Go Far, Go Together

There is an old African proverb that states *if you want to go fast, go alone. If you want to go far, go together.* I have been around sales teams that have had major distrust. They did nothing together and were backstabbing and did not trust one another. This is simply a miserable atmosphere. It is far better to have people working together, even splitting commissions at times, sharing in the growth of themselves and the company. One such team was struggling. The company brought in a new sales leader. The leader, we will call Joe, started to promote teamwork and reliance on each other. Joe encouraged each team member to start looking at their peers as ones who could provide help. Before long that team was changing their attitudes. Their peers weren't enemies and competitors but teammates. They were all going to benefit the more successful they would be as a team. That attitude goes far in helping one to be successful. The team went from a bunch of underperformers to becoming overachievers. Why do you think the turnaround took place? Was it because people perform better as a team?

Are there opportunities for you to partner up with someone? Maybe on the sales team there is someone that does something better than you. Perhaps you do something better than they do. Is there an opportunity to pair up and become a team in some circumstances? Maybe one is good with putting on events and the other is good at uncovering challenges a company or person may have. Could the person who is better at uncovering business problems go on a few appointments with the one who is challenged in this area? It sounds like each would benefit if there is some teaming up to work together.

What about some friendly competition? Is that a good thing? Most salespeople like a little extra incentive for winning some additional trip or reward. If the company is going to offer extra rewards for hitting some goals, there is nothing wrong with taking the prize money that's offered. It shouldn't pit us against our teammates though. Just like in a golf match, if your counterpart hits their ball in the woods, you would help them look for it right? By the way, it's not just golf, it could be a board game, cards, tennis, you name it. Friendly competition is the key for many in sales. Most of us like bragging rights occasionally.

SWD MASTER TIP

Salespeople can be team players. Find people who like to work together, Be helpful to others too. That can pay off. It can change a culture. Not only that, because of the team doing better, you will do better too. The stronger the team, the more sales will be, the more money coming into the company, which leads to more growth and stability and brighter futures for the employees. Teamwork does indeed make the dream work!

CHAPTER 16

Losing is Learning

"The number of times I succeed is directly proportional to the number of times I can fail, and keep trying!" ~Tom Hopkins

Some days will just not go well. Some opportunities will not go your way. You will lose. It does not mean you failed as long as you keep moving forward. Losing in sales is like losing in sports. In fact, there are tons of similarities in sports and sales. Thankfully, in sales, there is more than one champion! In sports, you do not win every time you step on the field or on the court. Michael Jordan, who many consider the Greatest of All Time during his years as a champion basketball player, said this: "I've missed more than 9,000 shots in my career. I've lost almost 300 games. Twenty-six times, I've been trusted to take the game-winning shot *and missed*. I've failed over and over and over again in my life. And that is why I succeed." Even the greatest of all time had to deal with losing.

Serena Williams is easily viewed as the greatest women's tennis champion, has won approximately 100 tournaments yet "lost" about 140. Her winning percentage has been off the charts but you can tell she is disappointed when she loses. Who cares though? People remember champions for their successes.

In baseball, a great player gets a hit about three out of ten trips to the plate. Ted Williams, one of the greatest of all time, averaged four hits out of every ten trips to the plate in one season. So six out of ten times, he made an out. If you get three to four wins in sales out of every ten opportunities, you may become an all-star too!

Great business people will lose opportunities as well. There will be times that you too will lose opportunities. The losses are not failures. Can you imagine any of these athletes saying they were a failure after a loss? I imagine they were more likely to analyze what they could have done better and committed to doing better the next time. Many athletes have very short memories. They may miss the game-winning shot one day and try it again the next with confidence they will make it. They don't stand and look at the goal and think, "I missed yesterday, I better even not try today because I might miss again." They get knocked down so to speak but they get back up!

Michael Jordan basketball extraordinaire said, "Obstacles don't have to stop you. If you run into a wall, don't turn around and give up. Figure out how to climb it, go through it, or work around it."

You are in the game. You will have your share of wins. Just understand that losing comes with the territory. It only means simply "not this time". The more deals and opportunities in which you are involved, the better. You only need enough wins to reach your goals. You will get there. The more opportunities you are in, the better your chances will be. Of course, we need to continue to improve our skills, but we will discuss this later.

In sales, we hear the word No probably more than any other profession. Studies show that the word No can have a negative impact on us emotionally. We don't like the word. In fact, we don't like to tell people No straight out. We will say things like "let me think about it" or "I will get back to you" or some other substitute to soften the blow of the word. Why are we like this? We know No can possibly hurt someone's feelings. We don't like it when our feelings are hurt. This is why many of us have hesitated to ask someone to go out on a date, or ask for a raise or promotion or whatever else, all because of the two-letter word "no".

Since we hear the word No in its many forms, it is a challenge to stay positive. There are tools available to help with the positive mindset. One is positive self-talk. We had on our Lead Sell Grow podcast, Doctor Shad Helmstetter, who is an author of over twenty books on self-help. His book *What to Say When You Talk to Yourself* and his SelfTalk Plus recordings will be helpful to put back some positivity into your mind.

We need to keep reminding ourselves, pretty much daily, that the word "no" does not mean no forever. No is "not now" or "not today". Unfortunately, many salespeople give up after the first "no" and they miss out on potential opportunities in the future. How many times have you walked out of a store with purchases after you told the salesperson you were "Just looking"? That "no" lasted only a few minutes!

I have experienced the emotional setbacks of the "no" myself. Looking back at one particular opportunity, I recall we were obsessed with winning a competitive deal in a high-profile account. What we were offering though had limitations and the client decided to go in a different direction. The doubt crept in for a bit. There was a great prospect with a keen eye and knowledge and they decided the competitor was a better fit. Did this mean that the competitor would be a better fit for everyone? Was I selling something that was inferior? The loss of the opportunity stung and then the negative thinking stung even more.

"Our greatest glory is not in never falling,
but in rising every time we fall."
-Confucius

What I had to do, was reflect on the happy clients that I had. Calling them after a loss just to see how everything was going and hearing how much they loved our solution, snapped me out of the funk. What we sell is not going to be a perfect fit for everyone. That is okay. There will be enough people who will think it's a perfect fit and you can earn a great living knowing this. Nothing will snap you out of the grasp of negativity like the reassurance from a happy client that you are indeed still amazing!

Just like in the wide world of sports, there is the wonderful thrill of victory, and unfortunately, the agony of defeat. These words were spoken every Saturday afternoon in the 1970s through the 90s by sports broadcaster Jim McKay. The video showed an athlete winning and celebrating as a champion and the next frame shows a skier who horrifically crashed down a long ski jump. On some days, you will feel like that skier. Search for "agony of defeat" on YouTube and you will see what I mean.

There are and will be many great days in sales with great wins to be celebrated. On those days you will feel like a champion. No one, no matter how awesome they may be, is going to win every deal or land every targeted account. There will be periods where you will have a string of successes, one after the other. You may feel invincible. You have arrived!

The wave doesn't stay up though. Waves do come down. Sales can at times feel like a roller coaster of emotions. Some great highs when everything is going well, and some low lows when nothing seems to be working.

Picture this, a prospect who promised to go with you has gone silent. She is not taking your calls. Finally, she picks up the phone and you can tell by the tone of her voice. It isn't cheerful like it was a few weeks ago.

She opens with, "I am sorry to tell you this…"

Instead of panicking, you realize that the timing wasn't right for this one perhaps. You lift yourself up. No does not mean No forever. You reassure the prospect. I am here to serve, you say. May I ask what the deciding factors were so I can improve for next time?

The Agony of Defeat, Then Victory

If you ever get a message on a Friday afternoon that you are winning the business, do whatever you can to get that deal signed that day. Do not say "I will bring over the paperwork first thing Monday. There are more than forty-eight hours where something could come up. I did this once. I have heard this before in my career. When people are ready, get the deal signed at that moment if at all possible. It is when the excitement and interest are the highest. I knew all of that. However, I was slacking on that Friday afternoon. I went into the weekend thinking I would have a nice deal to start off the upcoming week.

It was a rainy Monday when I went with my contract in hand to see the client. Who likes rainy Mondays? Nobody. But this rainy Monday was going to start off with this nice deal, so I thought. I walked into the business and saw the owner. I greeted him with a big smile and a warm greeting. There was no smile in return. He looked at me and said we can't do the deal. "I signed a better offer after I spoke to you. Your competitor came here on Saturday morning with an even better offer." I thought it was a joke. It wasn't. In that minute I felt "the agony of defeat." My rainy Monday became *really* dreary.

As much as it stung and how I felt about this person at that moment, I realized he did what he thought was better for his business. Within a few months, I was back in touch asking how everything was going. Before long, another opportunity came up and I tried again. I eventually earned the business this time around. I reminded the owner when I brought the agreement that I would stick around while he signed it! We had a laugh. I felt good. A no turned into a yes. I made the shot this time, nothing but net!

SWD MASTER TIP

In sales, you will get knocked down but you need to get back up. After losing and feeling down for a bit, I may put on a little music to get me out of a funk. I am sure my loud incredibly amazing voice was heard by some as I was singing/shouting, "I get knocked down but I get up again. You're never going to keep me down! I get knocked down but I get up again. You're never going to keep me down!" as I played Chumbawamba an all-time one-hit wonder.

Get used to the word no. It is only a word and it does not define you. No means "not today" or "not yet". Just like in baseball, we will swing and miss more than swinging and hitting. With each failure, we are learning. The lessons will prepare us to be better. In the beginning, you will lose more than you will win. Eventually, your persistence, practice, skill development, and being able to be yourself, will help you toward the goal of being successful.

CHAPTER 17

Show Them the Love

"I will greet this day with love and I will succeed." ~Og Mandino

This lady was all business. She was well dressed and on point while she spoke. She was the one who ran the company, one could tell. By her serious look, I knew she was a woman who knew what she wanted and small talk was not on her list of priorities for the day. If you know me, I like to build trust and get to know people. Yet, in this case, it was important to let go of the whole bonding experience and be completely in listen mode to the one who was taking charge. Instead of trying to offer advice or explain that I knew the technology and could help, I listened as if she was placing an order in the restaurant.

She was telling me how she wanted to buy. Although there was no bonding, I looked directly into her eyes telling her silently that I was there for her and she could trust me and eventually we would be friends. Yes, I say those words with my eyes when I look at people. Much is said through the eyes. I believed I would get the business because she must have had experiences with others who tried to bond early on and the one who worked with her in the way she wanted to work, would get the business. Indeed we did get the business after all. It was surprisingly easy once she told me how she preferred to buy.

Have you ever been in this type of "conversation"? Many who are in sales simply do not do well with people who don't fit their style of personality. They try to "break the ice" with people who hate ice. They want to bond with people who don't like to bond. When they get rejected, the person is viewed as a snob, jerk, or some other less than flattering description. It's easy to like people that are likable, and love those who are lovable. However, the world is made up of different types of people. Sometimes, we just struggle to get along with others who are different from us. How can we serve such folks who seem to be vastly different from us?

According to many of the personality profiles out there, there are four main personality types. We all fit at least one of them but can definitely have characteristics of the other three in us as well.

Just like our buyer above, the last thing she wanted to do is participate in meaningless small talk with salespeople. She greets you with a serious look which tells you to get to the point. What would you do? Would you look for pictures on the wall or desk of her family and try to bond?

What about this person, gregarious and loud. She is greeting and praising people as you head to her office. People are smiling at her and returning the greeting. She lights up the room with her energy and cheery disposition. She has pictures of people all over the walls and her desk. Behind her is the artwork of finger painting by a preschooler. She looks at you and smiles and asks, can I get you some coffee or a bottle of water? What would you say?

Here is another example. A person walks down the hallway toward his office. You mention a few words about the weather or the traffic to break the silence. He mumbles something back. People pass by in the hallway and there is no exchange of pleasantries.

Her office is pretty much barren. It is neat and all but no people's pictures are visible. She simply asks, "What do you have for me?"

Finally, there is this person. Charming and warm. She smiles at people and greets people but is not the loud gregarious type. Friendly and tranquil, She asks you how the traffic was as you are walking towards her office. She asks, what is on your mind today? How do you respond?

What have you observed from these four individuals? Would you treat them all the same? Which of these types would you prefer to work with? Someone that matches your personality? Most would pick the second and the fourth characters. They are "people" people. Most of us who are in sales prefer to work with these types.

What does that mean to you? Do you see any value in working with task-oriented people? Do you see any value in working with the decisive, somewhat demanding person? If you could work well with each type of person, what would that do for your income?

We probably have family members or relatives who have similar traits. They are regular everyday people who have different traits than us. It is that simple. Learning how to treat each, will go a long way towards developing trust. Since we are in the people business, it is in our best interests to be able to work with all types of people.

There is a personality assessment, DiSC, that has been around for years and can save you some time in trying to figure these personalities out on your own. There are combinations of personalities and the study can go far deeper than where we are going here.

D – Dominance – Driven by the bottom line, result oriented. Does not need to hear details. More task-driven
than concerned about people.

I – Influence – These folks are more open. Relationship
people that persuade and influence others. People over
task

S – Stable – They are dependable and sincere, peacemak-
ers. People over task and surprisingly introverted.

C – Conscientiousness – Think of people who like accu-
racy, data, and precision. Task before people. Introverted.

What job types can you think of for these individuals? Which
one fits the accountant or CFO? Which fits the business owner?
The HR manager? The IT person?

Now, which one would want all of the options and see spread-
sheets of data? Who would like to make a quick decision and
move on? Who wants to bond and get to know you as a person?
Who is the one that wants their staff to be happy but doesn't like
change?

Answers are: CDIS

So the ones that most salespeople do not get along well with are
the D and C types. The D is the cut to the chase person and the
C is the one that wants all kinds of data to make a very informed
decision. Where are the extroverts? D and I. The introverts are
generally the C and S types. Can we serve these types of people?
Are there any of these in your family? Can you treat them any
differently knowing the differences now?

SWD MASTER TIP

In order to do very well in sales, we need to be able to relate to people who are different from us. Some are introverts and love data. Others are pretty demanding and result-oriented. They don't want details and others do. Some like to bond and build up trust and others hate change. If we truly love people and work at helping them feel loved and important, we will be able to serve a wide range of people with dignity.

CHAPTER 18

People Buy Stories

"Marketing is no longer about the stuff that you make, but about the stories you tell." ~Seth Godin

The young boy took a hatchet and chopped it into a cherry tree. His father upon seeing the tree asked the boy what happened to the tree. The boy who apparently could not tell a lie told his father that it was he and his hatchet that damaged the tree. That boy received a big hug from his father who was happy that his boy was truthful.

That story was related to me as a kid by my mother to highlight the value of being honest. It was a fabricated story about a six-year-old George Washington written by an early biographer, Mason Locke Weems in 1806. The story made an impression on me and probably thousands of others over the past 200 years. When I thought of lying I thought of young George telling the truth about the cherry tree. That story, albeit fictitious, sold me on the value of honesty.

What stories do you recall from your youth? Do any of Aesop's Fables like the tortoise and the hare or the boy who cried wolf still remain in your memory? If so, you know the power of stories. Stories work well in sales too. Not stories about ourselves and our weekends and vacations, but stories about how others have benefitted from our services.

Think about the facts and statistics about smoking or seatbelts. Do those move people to change their behavior? Seeing a person with a story of how smoking caused them to get cancer or someone who lost a loved one who failed to wear a seatbelt stirs up emotion and is more memorable than statistics aren't they?

When I first started out in sales, I did not have any stories yet. I had information. I had some statistics and facts, but those did not stir up any emotion. As I accumulated experiences, those became stories for the next time when that topic came up. Telling stories can be a great way to build trust. People like stories if they are interesting.

Taking an experience where we had a successful outcome and sharing it with a similar company was the biggest reason for my success. One experience that stood out was a prospect who did not have the money for our "expensive printer". It was a defense contractor. We had plenty of success stories with similar companies, sharing the value of getting last-minute proposals for large government bids worth millions. However, this prospect was interested in our technology but was not moving forward in the sales process.

As they delayed in making a decision, an opportunity arose. They needed to get a bid out to a military base by a certain deadline. Since they depended on a quick-print shop to print these massive bids, they had to wait. They called, they cajoled, begged, and pleaded but they were not in control as to when the document would be completed. Frustration was mounting as the quick-print shop did not have the same urgency. Millions of dollars were at stake. Finally, as the documents were ready, there was no time left for shipping through FedEx or UPS. They had a choice, forget about the opportunity, or hire a private jet to fly across the country. In this particular case, they hired a private jet, which cost way more than our "expensive printer". Needless to say, we sold a printer within a few days of that experience. Is that a story that others could relate to? Every contractor depending on a print shop could relate to the story. That story sold. If this was your story, how many times would you have shared it?

Think of case studies. I should have made one about the private jet story! These are stories of how someone used a service and had a successful outcome. People like to read case studies if they apply to their business. (A hair salon case study is not going to apply to a law firm.) So they need to be applicable and relatable.

Our stories need to be concise, relatable, and relevant. Use imagery. Help them see it as if they are watching it on their flat screen. Tie the story into them and their business or life. If it is memorable for the prospect, you have done your job.

Stories Can Help Alleviate Concerns

We have all heard these before:
- The price is too high
- No budget
- It isn't a top priority/Too busy
- I'm not interested
- We currently are working with someone
- We're not in the market
- Send me some information

How we respond to these has a lot to do with selling with dignity. Sellers with dignity don't want to use pressure to sell. Stories sell. Relatability sells. Trust sells. Simply relating to a person who says something costs too much tells us either they are not a real prospect or they don't see value in the offer. Instead of saying something like, what do you mean by that or just acknowledging they said it was too much, can we do something else? Have we ever felt that something was too much and bought it and were happy with it? If we honestly thought it was too much, we probably felt like we overpaid. Is that relatable? Can you tell a story about not wanting to overpay?

What about paying more for quality? Is that relatable? Is there a story there to share? Maybe one that deals with paying less for something and then finding out shortly afterward it was less for a reason. Is there a story there?

When people say they are busy, can you relate? Do busy people become less busy in a month or in a year? No, they are always busy. Can you relate? Is there a story about how you helped a busy person by making things easy for them?

Are you getting the idea? Think of stories for each of the normal objections that you hear. Sometimes you may want to save the story until the person is more receptive. A follow-up call stating "you got me thinking" can rekindle the conversation and the prospect may be more inclined to listen as the pressure they felt at the moment probably has waned.

Stories sell. The founder of Christianity used stories everywhere. We know many of them including the prodigal son, the house built on a rock foundation, the sower of seeds on fine soil, to mention a few. These have lasted for over two thousand years. They were relatable, practical, and appealed to the emotions. They were more powerful than laws and data. The same is true with those who sell with dignity. For every occasion, accumulate the stories based on your experiences. Use them. Although you have heard the stories many times, your prospects have not. Stories sell. Become a storyteller.

CHAPTER 19

Communicate With Empathy

"To effectively communicate, we must realize that we are all different in the way we perceive the world and use this understanding as a guide to our communication with others." ~Tony Robbins

I like to just tell it like it is. Why beat around the bush or mince words? At least people understand me when I am direct. Have we ever said this or something similar? Many use these types of phrases in order to "speak freely". Yet even with asking permission, "is it ok to speak freely here?", (nobody says No to this question), are we sure that we aren't hurting feelings? The meaning of empathy in layman's terms is being able to walk a mile in their shoes. Do we try to understand fully how people feel when we are communicating with them?

While in the rural areas of the Dominican Republic (think of people living in wooden shacks with dirt floors), the locals showed incredible hospitality even though they were very poor by our standards. It was pretty common to be offered delicious-looking fruit juice made from mangoes, papaya, star fruit, and berries mixed with water. Maybe a lime would be placed on the rim of the glass. Sounds delicious right? On a hot tropical day, one can imagine how appealing this drink appeared to be. Unfortunately, in the rural areas, the water was not treated like it is in much of the world. Amoebas and other impurities cause quite a bit of aggravation if ingested. Many of us foreigners spent days and weeks recovering from bad water. I will spare the gory details but one would definitely lose weight as a side effect!

What is the lesson here? An invitation to drink was offered to us and within a second, we had to try to determine if our parched mouths from the dusty trails could be refreshed or not. Would we be able to look at this kind, generous, smiling, the person who was extending their hospitality to us and give an answer that was pleasant like honey?

We first tried pointing to the stomach and said the drink would make us sick in our broken Spanish. The look on their faces made us realize that was not a great response. Telling someone their hospitable offering would make us sick, went over poorly. This was a treasure they were offering us, made with love. They could drink it and tell us it was good. You see, their world and experience were different from ours. So we needed to think differently, putting ourselves in their shoes. How could we turn it down? Self-deprecation was the answer.

"We foreigners have weak stomachs. We can only drink water that is purified. One day, we will be strong like you." This made people laugh and it did not imply that we were not appreciative of their offer. This resulted in a win-win. We stayed healthy and they were not offended.

But the longer we were there the more chances we took. My wife reminds me of the stories of me having to make a mad dash back to the homefront, if you get my drift! (See a Seinfeld episode with Kramer percolating.)

As sales pros, we need to understand how to use words that

are pleasant for others to hear. We can send an unintended message by choosing the wrong words that are less appealing. Think of honey. You attract more flies with honey than vinegar. Sweet words are more persuasive than harsh ones. Being direct may cause some hurt.

Be careful with the honey!

Words being like honey implies that something is appealing. Just because it is appealing to us, does not mean it's appealing to others. Some love to talk about their company and the services they offer. How many of us have heard people say: "I am so passionate about what I do, I can't stop talking about it." They think because they are passionate about what they do, somehow translates that others are equally passionate. News flash~they aren't!

Others talk without taking a breath. It's as if they fear the pause. If they pause, maybe the person listening may express disinterest. So they keep on speaking in hopes they will eventually cover something interesting for the listener. They do this by painting pictures verbally or giving long soliloquies that are about as exciting as an eighty-page PowerPoint presentation filled up with twelve-point fonts. They do not work and they fail to communicate.

Don't be a walking brochure, the person showing up and throwing up features and benefits. This dumping of information only belongs in the dump. It is useless and alienating.

PowerPoint presentations that destroy brain cells. There is no better way to put this. Have you ever watched a presentation that is all text and bullets where the presenter turns their back on the audience and reads the slides? Is that communicating? The audience doesn't know where to look. It's a choice between the back and the untucked shirt of the presenter or squinting the eyes to try to read. Instead, we all get out the phones and catch up on clearing out old emails. *A PowerPoint deck should consist of the ten-twenty-thirty rule.* Ten slides. Twenty minutes. Thirty-point fonts. Even better, use pictures instead of fonts.

Hear What Isn't Being Said by Reading Body Language

Sometimes people are not completely open. Next time when you are meeting with multiple stakeholders, some will be actively listening, some may be sitting with arms folded and others may be distracted, even checking their phones.

What do we do with the different types of people here? It is our job to try to engage them. Ask individually what they think about what you are reviewing. What has their experience been in the past? What are they looking for now? These questions and others will help open them up and draw out their input. Again, this is a skill that needs to be developed.

The folded arms across the chest is another sign. It usually means they disagree with what is being said. Their mind is closed to what you are saying. Options here are to hand the person something to break up the folded arms. A glass of water, a brochure, a pen, can be offered. Also, you could reach out with your hand palm up and say "what's your thought?" and sit back.

We should be welcoming with open arms too. People will see us as sincere and trustworthy. I suggest watching Joel Osteen sometime and see how he warmly stands before an audience, greeting them. Then try this the next time you are at an event, tradeshow, or welcoming guests.

Facial Expressions

Have you ever seen a prospect or client's face and saw that they were not in a great mood? What did you do? Did you ever say something like "It looks like you have a lot on your mind. Would it be better to reschedule?"

Some may cringe at this idea because it is so difficult to get meetings. However, if the person is that preoccupied, what are the chances they will be present for your meeting? If they aren't present, how successful will the meeting be? Would it be better to give them thirty minutes or an hour so they can take care of the pressing need? What will that do for your relationship?

Another example, a prospect may be pleasant enough but is only giving short answers. Clearly, there isn't a lot of buy-in. Take a moment and mention that you appreciate the responses but I don't feel like you are convinced of what we have been sharing. What would you say we are missing? See if that draws the person out. Facial expressions are clues to what the person is thinking. Watch your own facial expressions too. People will see your genuine interest with your eye contact and facial expressions.

Smile Please

How important is a smile? Smiling makes us more attractive. People are naturally attracted to people who smile. Who would you rather approach, someone smiling or someone with a frown? Do we look happy and cheerful generally or like we just lost our best friend?

Studies have proven that when people smile, endorphins are released making people feel happy and less stressed. Our smiles make us appear happy. We are viewed as warm and kind when we are smiling and even more trustworthy! Aren't these the traits you want to express to others?

When we are smiling, we are communicating to others that we are happy people. Naturally, when the tone is serious, we don't want to be listening with a grin on our face. However, what do we look like when we walk into an office or a place of business? Are people referring to you as a happy, cheerful person? If they are, you must be smiling!

Less Than Great Communication

We should want to look, act and Be real professionals. There to serve and help people and be exemplary in our conduct. Here is a list of actions to avoid.

- Failure to look in the eyes when one is speaking to us
- Interrupting
- Checking your phone while someone is speaking
- Showing up late for meetings
- Being the loudest in the room
- Talking about yourself or your company without being asked
- Weak handshakes- We are not grasping an egg
- Overly firm handshakes- We are not in a strength contest

Think Before Answering Questions

Prospects periodically ask salespeople questions when there is interest. Salespeople by and large, respond immediately to the questions, without fully understanding why a question was asked in the first place. Isn't it true that a question may be asked for a reason different from what it appears to have been asked at first glance?

Think of the question that a woman may ask her spouse "does this dress make me look overweight?" That question is deeper than what appears on the surface right? Most of us who have been asked this, know that there may possibly be a reason for the question!

Some old sales trainers would say always answer a question with a question. This is an annoying practice. This back and forth is silly. Hopefully, we are not playing this game. However, when a person asks a question, we should understand the reason for the question.

We simply might say something like, "That is a great question. It sounds like you have had some experience with this in the past. Do you mind sharing a bit more about what is on your mind in order for me to better understand where you are coming from?" This type of question takes the pressure off the prospect and shows that you are trying to be empathetic and better understand them. This usually goes over pretty well. We all know the folly related to speaking without thinking. When being asked a question, we definitely need to be thinking before we speak and answer as if our words are sweet like honey.

SWD MASTER TIP

Good communication is key to being successful. Whether it be with the way we respond to questions, speak, use body language and facial expressions, communication is happening. Good communication is like a finely seasoned dish. It does not just happen naturally. It is not about telling others about ourselves and our services. It is all about the other person. What do they need? What are their true concerns? Understanding people and their challenges are what will help people to open up and trust you. Great communication requires effort. Keep working on it. It will not only help you in sales, but it will also help in all of your relationships. And please, remember to show your beautiful smile!

CHAPTER 20

Don't Fear "The Ask"

"If you are not moving closer to what you want in sales (or in life), you probably aren't doing enough asking." ~Jack Canfield

Unfortunately, due to the perception many of us have about pushy salespeople, we are afraid to ask for the order. The simple concept of asking for the business will be the difference between success and failure. Asking for the order can represent simply any step in the sales process. We need to ask for it and not look like we are being pushy for asking. Many would rather just keep the relationship as is, rather than risk losing the relationship altogether if the person were to tell us no.

Watching a video with James Muir, author of the *Perfect Close*, he says 50-90% of all sales encounters end without any commitment being asked. Can you imagine the potential here? (Get the book. It will not disappoint.)

Some will ask once, and if the answer is anything but Yes, the question may not get asked again. "Ask and it will be given to you." This implies that all we would need to do is ask once and *voila*, we will get what we are asking for. The key to success is to keep asking, tactfully of course, and being consistent over time. There is a huge need to be working in harmony with the desired Ask.

The Ask is critical to your success. We can be the best person for the job, the opportunity, the problem solving, etc. People will not read our minds. They will more likely think we are not interested enough to ask for the order. Suppose you worked in a company and they had a position they were looking to fill that paid more and was something you would be perfect for based on your skills. Would you apply for the position or just hope that your superiors would offer you the role without you asking? I am pretty sure if you wanted it, you would apply for it. You probably would approach HR and state that you are interested in the position. Is that being pushy? Clearly, it is not. If you want any position or role in a business, almost 100% of the time one needs to ask.

Asking for an order or the next step is like asking to be interviewed for a job posting you want. So many have failed in sales because they simply do not ask for the order. This asking is something we have done all of our lives from the time we asked for that very first cookie as a two-year-old. In fact, my two-year-old daughter would ask me if she could have two cookies or three. She knew that either option was a win for her.

The Shoe Shine Boys Made the Ask

In view of working in harmony for that which one is asking, let me take you to the Dominican Republic again. I am not sure if it's still true but in the late 1990s, young boys frequently earned income for the family with a shoeshine business. These troopers, often barefoot, traversed the streets looking for men or women with scruffy shoes and would ask to clean and shine them for a few pesos. These few pesos helped pay the bills. We felt bad for these kids as they were not able to live the carefree life many eight-year-olds got to live in other parts of the world.

They would go house to house or would walk down the city streets, with clothes, hands, and legs (they wore shorts) stained from shoe polish, looking to offer their services. In spite of the outside appearance they usually had big smiles and were quite friendly and conversational, as kids tend to be. For us, after having walked miles along dirt roads and trails, our shoes were ready for the trash bin. On more than one occasion the roads were so muddy that it was impossible to ride the motorcycle through some of them as the mud would glob up the tires. Sometimes the suction of the mud was so strong, we actually lifted our foot out of a shoe that remained encased in the mud clay. That was always worth a laugh, usually by someone watching us and chuckling at the crazy Americans!

On days like these, The boys would find us and point at our mud-covered shoes and say, "Aye sucio!" Much like we would say "yuck" emphatically indicating they really needed a shine. It really was pretty impressive to see what they were given to clean and what they handed back to us!

Selling is Solving

From the Shoe Shine Boys, one could learn a thing or two about this. First of all, they had an incredible attitude. The smiles were contagious and as curious kids, they would ask us questions occasionally about what we were doing there and why we had a hard time speaking the language. It wasn't long before we were calling them by their names and becoming friends with these little "entrepreneurs".

In our world of selling, we need to develop similar relationship-building skills in order to get people into the sales funnel. Don't deny the power of a smile. Like The Boys, are we smiling, bringing warmth and kindness to our potential clients? If we go through the day like we are forcing the effort instead of bringing positive energy to the world, can we expect to have the same results as the positive cheerful person? This is true whether in person, virtual or on the phone. A warm smile will help break down barriers.

The boys' chances improved after rainy days because the odds were in their favor that shoes were going to be muddy. They knew we had a problem, muddy shoes, and they were asking if they could solve the problem for us. Isn't that the essence of sales? Find people who have a problem and solve it.

The Shoe Shine Boys were tireless. Every day, they would ask for the order. They would occasionally be discouraged but, generally, if we said no one day, it would only be a matter of time before the shoes needed cleaning, and the "no" would turn to "yes."

You see, they would keep on asking. They did not just ask once and never return. A no yesterday on a sunny day would be different on a day after a rainstorm or a day walking the trails. No was not "no forever" it just meant "not now."

Frequently when speaking with a newer salesperson about the people they are calling on they will tell me that a person was rude, hung up on them, was mean, etc. The reality could have been simply that the person was not interested at the time and they had other things on their mind. Being tactful with a salesperson calling them while they were in the middle of doing something, simply did not occur to them. Does this mean we never should call on them again? No, of course not. The next time you call, simply state the last time we spoke you were pretty busy and suggested I call another day. Simple. Chances will be better the second and third time around once the prospect sees your persistence.

Buyers Choose Sellers That Ask for the Order

As an occasional buyer, I am amazed at the number of times that sellers have disappeared after making a presentation where I chose to wait instead of buying on the spot. I am sure that I am not alone. A person could have called on me a year prior but I am in the market now. I don't start looking through my emails trying to remember the person, I instead go to Google and search for companies that can solve my problem. If a salesperson is calling me or in contact with me regularly, she will get the first opportunity. The ones that stopped showing interest, miss out. All a salesperson needs to do is to stay top of mind with periodic emails or an occasional call. However, most do not do these little things.

SWD MASTER TIP

I suggest using casual non-threatening words to move onto the next step, an advance in the sales cycle. Simply saying would you like to *move forward*, or *start working* is much easier on the psyche than words like contract, order, and agreement.

All credit goes to James Muir for this simple to remember, yet brilliant question in *The Perfect Close* that I suggest you get comfortable in using: Does it make sense to...(fill in what is a reasonable next step)? If the person does not say yes, then say, "What do you suggest as a next step?" Keep on asking, as a wise man once said, you will eventually receive what you ask for.

CHAPTER 21

Negotiation ~ Make it a Win/Win

*"The ability to negotiate with other people without
friction and argument is the outstanding quality
of all successful people."* ~Napoleon Hill

Some people do not like to negotiate. However, negotiation is actually very common in our lives. Think of all of the times you discuss with your spouse or friends which show to watch, which restaurant to visit, where to vacation, where to live, or whatever else you may be deciding on. Perhaps you have differing desires on the choice of movie or the restaurant or vacationing in the mountains or the beach. In every relationship, there is a compromise, a give and take where each party benefits and sacrifices a little. As children, when we asked for some treat or privilege, we had to either have our homework done, our room cleaned, or make sure our chores were done. All of those were forms of negotiation.

What are the best outcomes for a negotiation? Isn't it the case when each party walks away from a negotiation and feels good about it, that we say it was a good negotiation? In healthy relationships, business partnerships, there is negotiation and compromise. Let's strive for our negotiations to always be a win for the buyer and a win for the seller.

I heard a funny closing line that was used by a young salesperson with a good sense of humor. When it came time to show the price he said something like this: I have two options for you. The first option, I will give a price that will be a bit high but we will go back and forth and negotiate and spend some time doing this. Eventually, we will settle on the price. The second option is my best price. Which option do you prefer? He said invariably people chose the second option. So the first option probably gets some people stressed a little but as soon as they hear the second option, they want to jump on that. I love the line myself. The humor is perfect for what could be a tense situation.

Early on in my career, I was given a verbal commitment from a prospect that they would be going ahead with our solution. After the customary small talk with the signer, the CFO, I pulled out the agreement and showed where it needed to be signed. He glanced at it and then said I was going to have to do better on the price. What did I just hear? The idea of being asked to drop my price had just not occurred to me!

This was my first experience where someone wanted to pay considerably less than the asking price. Between us friends here, I honestly didn't know what to do. My mind was racing. I recalled hearing other reps in the office say things like, "if I get to that price, will you sign?" To help you understand, dropping the price meant that the commission would be less. My pricing was more than fair. I was honest with my pricing and it was in line with what others were charging for similar technology.

I knew I had read something on negotiation but I was coming up empty with ideas. I was unprepared. Going forward, I would be prepared for curves being thrown but this is how one learns at times as we may be required to think on our feet.

I listened and finally said, "I came in with our best price and it's fair." That explanation was true, I did come in at my best price and hopefully, this would end the conversation and he would sign!

Unfortunately, it was not that easy. To help his cause, he brought in one of the stakeholders into the room. He started to ask the stakeholder, who we'll call Greg, questions to highlight why my price was too high. This is never going to end, I thought. My mind started to race again. What would I say? Would I know how to handle this? Then I reminded myself that Greg and I had some decent conversations during the selling process. I was curious as to what Greg would say and tried to stay calm and not panic.

The CFO questioned Greg, asking, "How is this technology compared to everything else we tested?"

"It was better," Greg said.

"But generally a printer is a printer, right?" the CFO asked.

"Well, not really." Greg went on to explain why.

"Didn't you say though that this wasn't as good in some areas compared to the others?" the CFO asked.

"Nope," Greg said. "We like pretty much everything about it and the support with Harry and his team."

As this turned out, it was clear that Greg was truly an advocate for us and he was actually doing the selling for me! The CFO at this point sheepishly looked at me and I did my best to keep a straight face. That was not easy to do as my smile felt like it was a mile wide! Needless to say, the negotiation turned out very well. I was able to keep the price as is and ultimately we both won. Our price was fair and in line with all of the competitors and they got what they wanted to solve their business problem. It really was a win/win. However, could I have handled it a little differently? Yes, and I will explain later.

The Close is Near

The first item about negotiation for me was recognizing that the signing of the deal was near. If people want to negotiate over price, be thankful. It is a sign they want to do business with you, usually. So with that in mind, it's a matter of recognizing that the prospect is looking for a better deal. Just like you, buyers want to feel like they are getting a "good deal". We all feel better about getting something off the asking price or some "freebie" that is thrown in.

Should we lower our price when someone asks? In my first year or two, I had the thought that lowering the price was unfair to those who paid the full asking price. So treating all fairly is what I tried to do. That does not mean selling everything at the same price. Look at all of the stores that have sales. A refrigerator at Home Depot may go on sale for several hundred dollars less than the normal price which can translate into a 20-30% savings or more. Home Depot isn't losing sleep over the fact that many of their customers bought the same refrigerator at a higher price.

In the above scenario with Greg, we set very fair pricing. It was the pricing that the market dictated. There is nothing wrong with the buyer asking for a better price or better terms for any agreement. They do it all the time. Since that first negotiation encounter, I would always try to have enough profit to allow for "wiggle room" when the price was being discussed. Giving *something* away like a little off the asking price, makes them feel better and you win too. Isn't that a win for both parties?

If you were selling bicycles for a living, would you sell them at the same price you bought them? Of course not. If the bikes are $500 and someone came in and said I want the $500 bike but I only have $300, would you sell the $500 bike now for $300? Of course not. You would show them a $300 bike if you had those to offer. The profits from the sales will help keep the store in business and pay for salaries and overhead. The same is true with whatever you are selling. You need to earn a living, pay for the expenses of your business, and whatever else is involved including all of the overhead. For some, selling with profit is a real challenge. Selling anything without sufficient profit is a recipe for disaster in the long term. This would be a temporary win for customers but if the business were to fail, the customer loses out too with a lack of support.

Who is the Better Negotiator?

Many who do the purchasing are very good at negotiating deals. Honestly, they are doing what is best for them and their company.

So they will at times offer a much lower price in hopes the salesperson will agree to it. They may ask for the world so to speak just to test us if we are willing to drop our price significantly. They are making us an offer and we do not need to say yes. Many untrained or unconfident salespeople do agree to the lower price.

One of the sales reps on our team struggled with selling with profit after numerous discussions and training. The purchasers would offer a much lower price and he would usually agree to it. He was afraid that if he did not meet their price request, they would choose another vendor. Because of this, he was barely earning enough income to make the job worthwhile. Those negotiations were a win/lose situation. The purchaser won but the salesperson really was not winning even though the sale was made.

Ask who the better negotiator is. How much training does the buyer need to say "I need it to be twenty percent less?" Are we trained to handle this price drop request? I sure hope so!

Do you have the reasons in your mind as to why you are not and will not be the lowest price? If you ever think you are charging too much, ask yourself:

- How much am I worth to the client?
- How valuable is the time I will be giving them?
- How much is my experience worth to assist them to get the most out of what they are buying?
- Will I answer the phone and respond to their emails in a timely manner?
- Will I stand up with them if there are any issues after the sale?
- Will I serve them well?
- Will I go the extra mile for them?

- Will I provide ideas that help them save money or earn more?
- Will I recommend them to other businesses?

If you answer "yes" to these questions, how much value are you bringing your clients compared to those who make the sale and move on? This may shock you but some salespeople do not return calls or emails after the sale is completed. Just because you care and will be there for your clients, you are worth more to them so you should charge more. People pay more for outstanding support, so give it to them.

The Take Away Close

One of my favorite lines for a "close" has been referred to as the *Take Away Close* over the years. It is simply removing the offer to see how the person reacts. If you are a parent, you have used this technique probably a few hundred times, especially when your child is less than appreciative of a gift. The words are: "this may not be for you" or similar.

An example of this is when a client of ours was in the market for new technology. He liked our support but shopped the price with a few other companies that offered similar technology. After finding a lower price, he came back to me and said, "I need you to match the lower price." He was saying the price was thousands less for the same exact product and was very direct with his request.

I did a lot for his business and I knew, he knew that as well. In response to his request for the lower price, I said, "That price is so low there is something wrong with it."

He then shared the quote to prove it was legit.

I looked at it and said, "Good luck with that."

He was stunned. "What do you mean?"

"We are not in the business to lose money," I said.

He was torn. I was taking our offer away in essence telling him to go elsewhere. The other price was substantially lower for the exact same technology. He knew our support though was really dependable and he relied on us. Was the lower price worth the risk of losing out on our support? The answer was no, that's why I am sharing the story.

Was there some compromise in the price? Yes, but it was minimal compared to what the competition was offering. He was playing hardball with me and I knew we had leverage and it was expected for me to play hardball back, which I did, and it worked out for both parties.

Another example of the Take Away is when a prospect seems to have lost interest. After some meetings, they may disappear for a bit. When they resurface again you might try to rekindle interest by going back mentally to where you last left off. If there is hesitancy you can say, "This may not be for you right now." No sense wasting your time if they simply aren't ready or able to do something at the present time.

Here are my 7 Keys for a Win/Win outcome:

1. Be prepared. Know your pricing and what you are willing to give up. Whether that be one percent, five percent, or nothing, know ahead of time.
2. Know why your prospect is buying from you. Keep going back to their goals and how you will be solving a problem.
3. Do not immediately accept a lower price if someone of-

fers. If they offer five or even twenty-five percent less, do not quickly say yes to get the business. That first request may be a test to see how willing you are to drop the price. Once they see you drop the price, a red flag may go up for them. The buyer may think if you reduced the price that easily on the first request, you will be willing to go even lower if asked again. Remember, the buyer is selling you on his desire to get the price down!

4. Do not be afraid to walk away from the opportunity. Most of the time, they will understand that you are serious and committed. (I was in a buyer committee meeting once and pushed my chair back and stood up and thanked everyone for the opportunity but I could not meet their price requests. I was invited to sit back down and walked away with the sale.)

5. If you drop your price, try to get something in return, longer commitment, removing some optional features, a testimonial, or something that also helps you.

6. Use the expression, "I will see what *We* can do." This puts the price in control of a team and takes the pressure off you. You may say this will take a day or so as it makes the buyer feel like you are taking them seriously but your counteroffer does not need to be what they were asking at all. Think about what your team wants. Then make the counteroffer with a positive voice knowing they are getting a Win too!

7. Stay calm, nobody is dying. You have done this before. Act like you WANT the sale but not like you NEED the sale.

SWD MASTER TIP

Negotiation is a *good* thing. It means the close is near and the client wants to work with you. Now it's your job to make sure it's a win for both parties.

Section 3
Own Your Destiny

CHAPTER 22

Say No to the Negativity

"When you're trying to achieve a goal, negative people will just bring you down. Surround yourself with the positive." ~Dave Ramsey

Think of yourself running to the finish line in the race to success. While others are running as hard as they can to win, you find yourself falling behind. Your legs are heavy and it's like you are running on soft sand. But wait, you realize there are weights on your ankles. You forgot to shed them after warmups. These aren't normal workout weights though. These weights actually have names, one is *The Downer* and the other is *The Drama King*. You need to shed them immediately!

Do you know The Downer? If you are unsure, here is an example of what they might say.

I am the person in the office that rarely, if ever, sees anything positive. I like to point out the negativity wherever I see it. I highlight what appears to be unfair. If someone is the boss's favorite, I will point that out. If someone is even speaking to the boss, they are trying to gain favoritism, and I will be telling others about it.

The new comp plan, well you can count on me to highlight the negative. New person onboarding, I will let them know how it really is here and who is already looking for a new job. I will congratulate people but give snide remarks behind their back.

I give phony compliments to the boss and mock praise to make myself look good. I may wander by your desk to see if there are any accounts you are working on that I might know. I might say I am already working on that one or I know them there, don't waste your time.

New sales strategy? Are you kidding? What I have been doing for years is just fine. That new strategy will fail, you will see. To them, LinkedIn is a fad. Phone calls are useless. Emails won't get read. They are negative about everything.

Avoid The Downer. That person or a group of Downers as they sometimes run in a pack will ruin you. Negativity has no room in our lives. To be a selling superstar you must remain upbeat and positive. Sure we will have doubts and challenges periodically but the key is to find the positive side and focus our energies on that. These negative nellies are there to test us. Are we able to persevere and overcome the adversity they may heap on us? To be sure, we must see the line, and instead of wandering over to The Downers den, we must remain focused on our business. It's much better to be putting our energy towards growing our business versus getting dragged down to their state of complete misery and failure. The Downers love to see others fail too. They don't want you to succeed and they will talk behind your back if you do. They need to go and find something else with which they can be happy, but that is not your concern.

I have seen The Downer destroy the morale of a team. They ridicule everything about the company, the compensation plan, the sales leaders and are mentally checked out. Their joy is not being successful but it's in tearing others down to make themselves look better. If the Downer has been around for a while, why are people putting up with the negativity? Frequently it's due to The Downer being a consistent producer. But that type of production is not good for the overall health of the company.

Unfortunately, The Downer is not alone. The Busybody is The Downer's close friend. The Busybody is also known as The Drama King (or Queen). Instead of doing the numerous activities that a great selling superstar will do, the Busybody wants to interrupt you from your day so they can talk about silly office gossip. The Busybody needs to be avoided as well.

How anyone would find more joy in gossip, drama, and negativity than look at their opportunity to make a great income and work toward that income, is beyond me! I have seen these bad apples throughout my career periodically. They will find others like them in the company. It's like they speak code somehow and they recognize the negative vibes in the ones that share their outlook. Beware, they like to meet for lunch too. If you join in the lunch crowd one time and they are that open to speaking pure negativity in front of you, know that this is something with which they are unashamed. Avoid them like the plague. Their spots will eventually show and they will be given the warning to shape up or ship out. However, that's not your problem.

I have had salespeople ask me what to do when people in the office try to interrupt them and go down the negative, gossip, or drama path. Just as you make eye contact with people you care about, do not stop what you are doing nor give them any eye contact. You have no time at all for them. They will get the hint. If you need to be more clear you can say that you have to focus on my business right now. That will get it done. Besides, remember your hourly wage is somewhere near $50 an hour. Would you give $50 to stop what you are doing to listen to the drama nonsense?

Definitely no!

SWD MASTER TIP

Jay Shetty in his book *Think Like a Monk* talks about this very topic of negativity in the workplace. We all know that gossip is not healthy yet many of us fall into the trap. For a former monk, he realized that gossip was not for him. The answer? Highlight something good about the person about whom the rest were gossiping. Eventually, they got the point and when Jay was around, the others would not gossip. Being a Busybody or Drama King or Queen, are not traits for winning. You have a job to do. Becoming a superstar sales executive on a mission requires focus and to be steadfast. Do not hold onto these people as friends just as the runner sheds the warm-up weights. Make your business a drama-free zone!

CHAPTER 23

Master Your Craft

"Unless you're continually improving your skills, you're quickly becoming irrelevant." ~Stephen Covey

Have you ever been to an art festival to see the amazing work that creative talented people can create? Think of the detailed paintings that almost appear as if they were a photograph, or the elegantly carved woodwork or the beautifully crafted artwork out of some type of metals that blow the imagination. If art is not your thing, consider an athlete who has mastered a sport that you have played. Maybe it's golf. Many of us play the game but the ones that master it, well, the way they play is on a whole different plane than the rest of us. What about musicians, well it takes about seven years at two hours per day to become an expert guitar player. So the next time you hear someone say I wish I could play the guitar, you can remind them that all it takes is the time to put in the effort.

What do these artists, athletes, and musicians have in common? Were they naturals that could just pick up a brush and paint or swing a golf club and be an expert at it? Or did they have to work on the craft? Do you think everything comes easy for them? Granted, some may have better hand-eye coordination or are "gifted" to some degree, but in order to get to the top, they need to practice and develop the skills. There is a saying which describes this very well, "*Hard work beats talent when talent fails to work hard.*" In other words, practice is more important than natural talent.

How many paintings ended up in the trash or were put away in an attic because they weren't good enough? How much practice is required in order to excel at the game of golf? Are you ready? It is not unusual for pros to practice ten hours per day, six days a week. That is *practice* folks! How many of us have that type of dedication? I dare say that it would be a very low percentage of the population.

What does this all mean? Practice is required to become great at anything. We may not enjoy it as much as the actual "game" but if we want to excel, we need to work on the craft of selling. Some, when they start in sales, think that all they need to do is to know a little about their product and share it with people. When they do that, they are a salesperson, so they think. I beg to differ. We can have a job in sales, but that does not magically make us a skilled salesperson, one who excels. When it comes to golf, I have played for decades and am a mediocre player. Why? Because I had a fixed mindset and stopped practicing years ago. I was talented enough to compete on the high school golf team but haven't advanced since then. I failed to recognize the need to continue to work on the game. The same is true with many salespeople. They are still at the same level with a fixed mindset as when they first started. They are playing their first year over and over again twenty or thirty years later. They are still talking more than listening, still lacking business acumen, dropping prices like that's the only option, afraid of trying new ideas, and wonder why sales are getting harder and harder to come by. Silly isn't it?

SIDE BAR

I am not proud of this story. Thankfully I learned that cutting off one's nose to spite the face is not a good decision. Regarding the golf team story, there is more. I was happy to be on the team competing. But I was having a few bad rounds and I was benched. Instead of buckling down and working harder, spending some extra time on the practice range, I let my own foolish pride get in the way. I told my coach that I was going to quit and focus on work. He was stunned and said I was making a mistake. He was right. The team went on to win the state championship. I was not there. What was the lesson? Do not let pride ruin your potential. That was a life lesson. I recommend whenever faced with making a decision based on pride, talk it over with a close friend or family member. They may save you some pain and agony that could last for years. By the way, that decision to quit based on pride was one that instead of looking back at that and being grateful I faced a challenge head-on, I am grateful for learning a lesson on the foolishness of ego and pride.

I Have Arrived

Have we ever worked out in a gym or exercise to tone up for a period in our life? Doesn't it feel great to look in the mirror and see that we lost weight or put on some muscle and can fit in clothes that we outgrew? Is that trim appearance easy to maintain? What happens after we stop exercising for a few months or years? Do we continue to have the firm muscles and trim look or do we start to soften?

Some who are in sales, think they are still fit and trim when they look in the mirror but in reality, have not exercised their brain in years. They think they have arrived and do not need to develop any longer. Is that really the case? Think of all the careers out there that require constant training and education in order to stay on top. Do dentists, doctors, nurses, counselors, attorneys, scientists, engineers, teachers have to continue to learn about their craft? Of course, they do. As new technologies, new ideas and practices become available, wouldn't someone who is on top of their game, want to learn about these? There are always changes and new challenges to which one needs to adapt. In the beginning, most of us are shocked at how difficult it is to get people to listen to us when we have a shiny new object or service to sell. So yes, we have to deal with this reality and learn to improve. However, the rewards are great if we work at it and stick with it.

A golfer doesn't just practice on one aspect of the game. They practice with wedges, drivers, short chips, putts, sand shots, shots from the rough, long irons, short irons, you get the idea. We need to know about our product(s) and how they solve problems. Shouldn't we be able to give expert advice as a salesperson or will superficial knowledge be enough to make a great living? If we are selling to businesses, what do we know about business in general? Do we have business acumen automatically or do we need to learn that as well?

What about people? What do you know about the various personality types and how to relate to them? There are people that need all kinds of data to make a decision. There are others that get overwhelmed with data and just want to know what they need to know. There are people who were taught to dislike and not to trust salespeople. How will you work with these? Some will want to laugh and have fun with sales reps during the buying process and others will be deadly serious. How will you relate to people who are not at all like you? *(See Chapter 17.)*

What other areas do you think you need to learn about and stay sharp? Have you ever been to a doctor or a dentist and it felt like you were walking back into the past? Everything was outdated and discolored and nothing looked even close to new. Would you trust that this "professional" was on top of their game?

With all of the advances in technology and the various platforms that people are on, potential clients can be found on Facebook, LinkedIn, YouTube, TikTok, Instagram, and other sites. Would you say that it would be helpful to understand these and learn to use them or would you be like the old doctor in the office that hasn't bought into newer technology and is content to stay in the past?

We all have opportunities to learn and stay sharp or improve. Whether it be podcasts, books, Kindle, YouTube, there are educational tools for sales everywhere and in whatever medium that we prefer. Years ago salespeople who were stuck in their ways would say they weren't much of a reader. Now they would have to say they aren't much of a listener or a watcher either. We can all spend some time watching videos, listening to books, and taking what we learned, practice and record ourselves.

Practical ideas include listening to a valuable podcast on your way to a sales call or your commute. Find a few Sales authors or gurus on YouTube and subscribe to their channel. Watch something for fifteen minutes a day. Connect with teachers or follow them on LinkedIn or Facebook. There you will have opportunities to see their posts and possibly join one of their webinars.

Should you invest in anything that costs money for training or education? Or should you have the attitude that it is not your responsibility to pay for the advancement of your career in order to earn more for you and your family? If it's not your responsibility, then whose would it be? If a doctor, dentist, engineer, counselor, attorney or you pick the professional, need to take a class, who do they expect to pay for it? Yet some salespeople think otherwise. Do not be like them. Invest in yourself.

What about hiring a coach? You may not even know about this option. Can a coach help you to become better at your craft? Do you think there is any professional athlete these days that does not have a personal coach? A coach will help you determine where you are today and will help you get to where you want to go. Is it worth the investment? How much more income will you earn by becoming more skilled at your craft? It is not unusual for sales professionals to move up the ranks into sales leadership, VP of Sales, and even company presidents who come from the sales ranks. The financial opportunity can be tremendous.

An MBA can cost upwards of $50,000.00 US to $100,000.00 as of 2020. People make this investment to get further along in their career to earn more than they could without an MBA. Now, there are many many folks with MBAs that have gotten more than their investment many times over by the advancement of their career.

But there are many others who spend that money and do not earn near the amount a skilled salesperson can earn. Some go to school for ten years and do not earn what some earn selling. Amazing isn't it? However, these top earners did not get there without practice and coaching along the way.

What did you learn from this? Having a sales job does not make one a skilled salesperson. One can get to the top in sales by working at the craft. It takes real effort. Most are not willing to put in the effort and therefore struggle and they keep looking for a better product to sell. With you, will it be different? Will you put in the time? Will you practice? Hire a coach? Make yourself better? Become an expert? It's all up to you!

SWD MASTER TIP

Not everything needs to be done in one day. Imagine that you start listening to educational audio whether it be books or podcasts on your way to work or in the gym during your workouts. Start doing this daily for a month and see what it does for you. Take a class on how to use LinkedIn for your business. Think about learning how to write great emails. All you need to do is google that. Hubspot has enough valuable ideas in their sales blog to last a lifetime on their website. Start with the audio for a month. Then add LinkedIn training for a few hundred dollars. Emails can be improved with a couple of articles. Before long, inside of a year, you can be much further along than where you are today. As the famous quote attributed to Lao Tzu says: "The journey of a thousand miles begins with one step." Looking back, you will not believe how much progress you have made over time. Little by little, improving each day, you will get there!

CHAPTER 24

Keep Your Word

"Your word is your honor. If you say you're going to do something, then you need to do it." ~Joyce Meyer

Keep Your Word

Doing the right thing is a huge part of treating others the way you want to be treated. It is the Golden Rule in common language. I have viewed sales as a relationship experience where people learn to trust each other as buyer and seller and are doing what's right towards each other. This is the ideal. Unfortunately, this is rarely the case.

Many salespeople make all kinds of promises in order to get a deal signed. Once the deal is signed, it is not unusual for the promise-making salesperson to do a disappearing act. They promise gifts, special treatment, business referrals, unlimited training sessions, lunches at great restaurants, but then none of it comes to fruition. A bunch of empty promises were made.

Have you ever heard the expression, "under-promise and over-deliver"? What is the spirit behind this expression? Is it to make a few promises and then over-deliver on doing favors for the client? Or does it simply mean don't make a bunch of empty promises but deliver on your word and keep your commitments?

An example might be a sales rep who promises to be very visible post-sale, provide unlimited training, take the team out for lunch, etc. None of it happens. The client feels like they have been deceived, and they have been. They email the rep without a response. They try calling but the voicemail is full and they can't leave a message. This is why many dislike salespeople. Unfortunately, until we prove otherwise, they think we will do the same.

The Bait and Switch

Have you ever been lured into a superstore because you saw an advertisement that had a ridiculously low price on it? What happened when you arrived? Were you told that the particular model is not available but we have others? Of course, the others are higher priced. That is the bait, where they lured you in, and then it was switched to something more appealing to the seller.

This is pretty common and people have their guard up for it. Things may happen after we get an order. Maybe something was said about the delivery time frame that can't be met due to some unforeseen circumstance. What can you do? How can you keep your word? Take care of this client. If you give them your word, do whatever you can to keep it.

Word Kept, Word Not Kept

Early on in the sale process, we can show the prospect that we are trustworthy. Let's imagine the prospect has a sheet of paper with two columns. On the left column it says Word Kept and on the right, it says Word Not Kept. Every time we say something trustworthy they put a check in the Word Kept column. We can say things like I will call you first thing in the morning to give an answer to your question. If we call by nine am, a check goes into the Word Kept column. We may say we will send a follow-up email by the close of business. When we hit send before five pm, we just added a check in the Word Kept column. However, if we call at eleven am, it is no longer the first thing. If we can't get to the email by five pm but send it the following morning, we lose a little credibility and the check goes into the Word Not Kept Column. The goal is to have all checks in the Word Kept column. If you are unsure if you can keep a commitment, don't make one. It is better to not commit than to commit and not do it.

If we have plenty of checks in the Word Kept column, we can be forgiven when things do not work out as planned and we can't keep our word as we would like. Some things are out of our control. All we need to do is to apologize. If we can't get the response by close of business as promised, simply apologize and do not blame anyone else. You may not get the check in the Word Kept column, but it may prevent a check from landing under Word Not Kept. Word of caution, if we are making commitments and not keeping them with any consistency, we are showing we are not trustworthy. The apologies quickly lose all meaning.

The greatest benefit of having plenty of checks in the Word Kept column is we are going to be viewed as *trustworthy*. When you do the right things, you are building your reputation and brand. You will be recognized by others as one who can be trusted and will always honor their word. Your clients will happily recommend you to others as one who can be trusted. When the buyer leaves one company and goes to another, they will remember you. People will want to do business with those that "do the right thing" just as you would.

All we need to do to build trust is do what we say. Whatever we say, stick with it. If we make a commitment and keep it, we are building trust. If we break our word or our commitment, we are breaking the trust. The more checks we have in the Trust column, the better it will be for us and our clients. Keep your word and do what you say you will do. It's that easy!

CHAPTER 25

Make it Memorable

"Do what you do so well that they will want to see it again and bring their friends." ~Walt Disney

This is about all you need to be successful in sales and business. If one can master how to treat others, then they will undoubtedly be successful. Think of the Uber driver that is offering water, mints, choice of music, choice of conversation or silence, the hand sanitizer, newspaper or magazine and has a spotless car inside and out that has the fragrance of cleanliness. Will you want to ride in their car again?

What about the restaurant that treats you like royalty? It does not need to be a fine dining Michelin restaurant in order to experience outstanding treatment. The server at the local diner asks for your name and before long you are walking in the door and hear your name called out. They learn what you like and treat you like family. What makes you go back? Is it the food or the experience?

The experience you provide for your clients will either get you repeat business and referrals or it will be shopped every time. Some salespeople are viewed as the devil that is known is better than the devil that isn't. But the door is open for an honest, caring individual to take over that business. Most salespeople do not think about the client experience from the moment they meet them. Everything is about closing. They are thinking of themselves and the commissions they will earn, not of their client. From the first phone call to the appointment to follow-ups and proposals, the client experience is never considered. The salesperson may be nice enough and friendly, but they are "forgettable" unlike the experiences above. Do you want to be like everyone else or do you want to be *unforgettable*? Unforgettable experiences will build a solid reputation and growth.

In sales and business, every interaction could begin with "how would I like to be treated?" Granted, it is not easy to do this but we should at least consider areas where we can improve. Most do not even know where to begin. They don't consider the client experience as part of their overall strategy. But what about you? Is there a way to consider your client's experience and how they are experiencing doing business with you?

- Phone calls - Be pleasant and upbeat
- Emails - Keep them concise and to the point, no rambling
- Casual conversations - Show genuine interest in them
- The down-to-business conversations? Do you transition nicely and pay attention to the details?
- The offer? Are you explaining it and providing options if applicable?
- The treatment you provide after an offer is made? Are you polite or a pest?
- How does the contract get presented? Is it neat and clean? Handwritten like the 1980s or neatly typed?
- What about post-sale? Are you keeping the client informed? Are you providing what they need in order to

use what you provided, effectively?

- Are you sending thank-you notes?
- Providing little treats for the staff if applicable?
- Participating in their charity somehow? Sometimes it is as simple as donating a few dollars to a 5k run or offering a little gift card for a fundraising event.
- What else comes to mind with what you are selling to help make the experience unforgettable?

I have been around a lot of salespeople and did business with countless companies over the course of my life. There are very few that provide memorable experiences let alone unforgettable experiences. If you do, you will never lack business. Even if you are starting out, what if you sent a simple thank you email every step of the way through the sales cycle? Could you thank people for the first conversation? Could you send a thank you email after the first meeting? The demonstration or the assessment? After the sale maybe send a nice card or something a little more special depending on the size of the opportunity. When one buys a house or a nice car, the gift may be a little more than something that is far less in cost. It doesn't have to break the bank but a $50 gift after someone spends tens of thousands with you is a nice gesture, if it is allowed. (Some clients can't accept gifts but maybe you can do something for their staff or their charity)

Michelle, who has been successful for years in providing a nice client experience is a good listener. A prospect who was considering us as their vendor brought up the fact that their CEO enjoyed giraffes and had little sculptures and carvings of them in his office. After a few months passed and the prospect became a client, Michelle did not forget the giraffes. She ended up spotting a very nice little figurine in the store while she was shopping. Her mind flashed back to the CEO in this account. She bought the giraffe and the next time she visited the client, asked if she could meet the CEO for a few minutes as she had a little gift for him. Once he saw the giraffe he was pleasantly surprised by the gesture. The CEO then told her that many salespeople have come into his office over the years and saw the giraffes and made empty promises about adding to his collection. He told her that you never even made the promise, you just did it. This is how under-promising and over-delivering works!

The questions above are for the client experience. What about your internal client? Again, the style of many salespeople is to ignore the team around them and talk about "I and Me" instead of "Us and We". The people around you want to be treated well and fairly too. What can we do to help their experience of working with you? Do we ever ask "is there anything I can do for you?"

SWD MASTER TIP

It is all up to us. We can provide incredible experiences for our clients that are truly unforgettable. Start to build habits with thank you notes and cards. Then add to these. Your reputation will grow and you will be one of the few salespeople that others will recommend without you having to ask for referrals.

CHAPTER 26

I Am A Winner!

"Whatever the mind can conceive and believe,
it can achieve." ~W. Clement Stone

What was the most amazing thing you have done so far in your life? It doesn't have to be climbing Mt. Everest or something like that. It could be that we learned to speak another language or learned to play an instrument and got the job over dozens of applicants. Whatever the amazing thing was, did you see it in your mind first? If we see it first, we can turn it into reality.

What does it mean to move mountains? Sometimes the challenges really do seem to be as large as mountains. Yet we overcome the challenges when we have the desire to do so. Throughout history, humans have done some amazing things. The mountain that appears before us can be climbed if we have the desire to do so. Looking back, I bet you see a number of mountains that you already traversed!

Throw the Head Trash in the Trash

Think about this crazy thought. Sometimes the best selling and buying goes on in our own heads! Our minds may be full of negative self-talk with all kinds of crap as to why we can't do something or pursue our dream. Let's not buy what our negative mind is selling. Instead, let's take charge of this particular sales cycle and re-sell ourselves that we are fully capable of pursuing our dreams and reaching our goals in life.

Maybe it's because we compare ourselves to people who might do something better than us. Or perhaps we have grown accustomed to belittling ourselves when we make a mistake. I know I have done this. How does this practice of even jokingly beating ourselves up, help us? It really doesn't help. In fact, we start to believe this nonsense. We all have our own unique gifts. So from now on, let's remove these phrases from our vocabulary:

- I'm a failure
- I stink at this
- I'm not outgoing enough
- I don't deal with rejection well
- I knew this wouldn't work
- I am not aggressive enough
- I don't do well with people
- I don't like to fail
- If it doesn't work out I will just quit

Have we ever said any of these and expected to succeed at whatever we were doing? Imagine learning to ride a bike and saying some of these statements. What would have been the chance to succeed?

Think of something you have done well. Whatever it is, whether it be playing a sport, doing well in a certain class in school, a certain hobby, what was your attitude about it? Did you quit after a bad day? Did you think that you stunk at the activity because something didn't go as planned? You finished school, learned how to read, cook, drive a car, enjoy hobbies, and hundreds of other activities. With all of these on your resume, you are a proven winner already!

Visualize and Attract

If you took a hammer and some nails and some boards and just started hammering nails in blindly, would you expect to build anything of value? Obviously, the answer is no. What do you need to do first before you start building anything? We need a picture or a drawing before we start cutting away or hammering nails in randomly.

If you are making a certain dish and have a recipe book with pictures, do you see the dish before it is created in your mind? If you are creating a painting, do you have an idea as to what it will look like before you start?

What do our answers show with these questions? Before we start, we need the vision first. Yes, sometimes we have to start a little bit but then eventually we need the vision before the project is completed.

Before you take a vacation to the beach or mountains, what do you see in your imagination? You visualize yourself on the beach, smelling the salt air, listening to crashing waves, feeling the sand between your toes, and looking out over the beautiful blue ocean. Similarly with the mountains. You visualize the green trees, the rocky trails, streams of cool water, sounds of birds chirping, incredible views from cliffs, all in your imagination.

Visualization is very common with us, once we think about it. The same is true with sales. Granted, it may take us a bit to get the visual down, but we should work on it early. In my case, I was in the Dominican Republic sitting on a veranda overlooking miles and miles of green mountains and valleys with scattered palm trees. In that scenery, I saw my future self in a car with a laptop computer en route to businesses, to sell technology. Twenty-five years later, I still see that view from the veranda.

When speaking with prospects, we also want to see them buying from us. We want to visualize the happy client that loves us and welcomes us. Like long-lost friends, they are happy to see us when we meet with them. Even if something goes wrong, our vision is that person smiling and thanking us for fixing whatever the problem was. You will be amazed at outcomes if you visualize or see them beforehand.

Positive "I AM" Affirmations

I AM amazing! I AM amazing! I AM amazing! Have you ever said these words? If so, how did you feel when you repeated this phrase? Do the words make you smile? Do they help you to feel a little more confident? When you walk into work or into a meeting, do you say "I hope I do well" or do you say "I AM amazing!"

What is the difference between saying I AM amazing compared to saying I will be amazing? It is sort of like the sign at the pub that says *Free Beer Tomorrow*. Do they ever give away the beer for free? Nope. Because tomorrow is never today. You are amazing today!

When we say who we are and how we are in the present, it is more powerful. We are telling ourselves that we are, instead of postponing it down the road to a day that never arrives. I am a business owner. I am a salesperson. I Am attractive. I Am fun. I Am loved. I Am fit. I AM bright. I Am a winner. Do we get the idea? Otherwise, if we push things off to the future, we don't have to Be a certain way now. If we were to say someday I will be fit, does someday ever come? The iconic band of the 1960s CCR, has a song that is titled, *Someday Never Comes.*

I AM a super helpful, people-loving, problem-solving, sales superstar. Try saying these words. Do they make you smile? What will happen if you say these words several times throughout the day? Maybe you put them on a sheet of paper in the bathroom mirror so you see them every day. How much better will you be thinking you are amazing versus mediocre?

Who of us thinks it a good idea to tell ourselves things like: I am nobody, I am useless, I am dumb, I am overweight, I am ugly, I am a failure, I am a scatterbrain, I am always late, I am terrible at math, I am bad with names, I am too old, or whatever other negative thing that comes out of our mouth at times? Saying these things is a bad idea, right? So let's stop saying them and replace the negative with the positive!

I AM a valuable human being created by God. I AM useful and helpful. I AM smart. I AM fit. I AM attractive. I AM successful. I AM organized. I AM punctual. I AM great with math. I am great with names. I AM young. Just as being negative makes us act negatively, what will positive thinking do for us?

SWD MASTER TIP

Our belief in what we can't see, except in our mind, can help us reach just about any goal or overcome any obstacle. Visualizing the outcome before we set out, will help us to achieve what we conceive and believe. Instead of thinking and saying negative thoughts, let's state the positive. No name-calling if we make a mistake. Use the I AM affirmations regularly. With these and visualization, you will be... (scratch that), you are amazingly successful!

The Wrap Up

So What Did We Learn?

We all find ourselves in situations in life where we are less than comfortable. Just about every woman can understand the feeling of being uncomfortable when she needs to take her car to a mechanic because her car is making a strange noise. Will she be treated with dignity and respect or will the mechanic view her as an opportunity to make some extra money by making unnecessary "repairs"? Or a guy who is looking for something special for the woman in his life and needs to visit the women's department at Macy's. In order to get the gift, he has to overcome the discomfort. Getting comfortable with what is uncomfortable is something we have done many times in our lives. The first day at a new school, new job, meeting strangers at a gathering, we have all done it and still made it through these challenges alive somehow!

Selling and keeping our reputation as nice, honorable people is also something that we can do. We don't have to compromise principles or character to sell our services. Serving is what drives us. We put others' interests ahead of our own. This is what people want, isn't it? Jim Rohn once said, "service to others leads to greatness." Zig Ziglar said to "stop selling and start helping." The actions of serving and helping will get us further in the sales profession. Now granted, we need to earn a living in our service in business and we can be like the professional server in the upscale restaurant. They serve and *they sell* by listening to their customer, understanding their goals, and then providing the product and service they desire. Selling is pretty much the same. We listen to our prospects, understand their needs and goals, and then offer to serve further with a product or service that solves their problem.

Do we have a Giver's mindset? Giving to give is different from giving to get. Giving and expecting something in return is not giving. Givers don't worry about the payback and aren't keeping score. Doing what is right will have beneficial outcomes. Where can we give? Do we share our insights with people freely? Do we put out content that is valuable and free? Gary Vaynerchuk lays this concept out nicely (language warning if you look him up). He tells his audience to give, give, give, give and then eventually make an ask. Eventually, some may want to do business with you. The more you share, the better it will be for your audience and friends and in turn, you.

As business owners and owners of our own destiny, our future depends on us. Knowing the numbers will be of great importance. Some businesses fail simply because of not knowing the numbers. How many clients do we need to reach our goals? How do we get those clients? What will it take from us? Speaking with one client who spends significantly on websites and marketing, only needs a few clients in order to reach her financial goals. She could feasibly reach those goals by being involved in the right networking or Chamber of Commerce events to meet those potential clients. So before we spend tons of money on websites and marketing, do we really understand the numbers?

This ties into the relationships we have built up over the years. Who knows us? People prefer to do business with the ones they know and trust, friends you might say. The more relationships we have, the more opportunities we will have. Harvey Mackay sums it up, "Business is all about building relationships!" Add that with Dale Carnegie's line: "You can make more friends in two months by becoming interested in other people than you can in two years trying to get other people interested in you."

The traits of persistence and patience are what we need to develop. The cliche Rome was not built in a day does apply in business as well. We need to not only do the right things, but we also need to continue doing them. Thomas Edison, one who knew a lot about persistence, said "our greatest weakness is in giving up". When do you buy items? When someone asks you to buy or when you actually have a need? Your clients think similarly. They buy when they are ready, on their timeframe, not ours.

Whether we are introverts or extroverts, we can succeed if we listen to others and show we are interested in them. The famous quote from Dale Carnegie should be burned into our mind, "To be interesting, be *interested*." If we show we are interested, they may find us interesting as well. It isn't about telling others what we do that makes them remember us. It is the empathy, care, and love that they feel from us that makes us memorable.

Eventually, we need to make The Ask. What did we learn from the smiling shoeshine boys? They asked repeatedly. No means simply "not today". Let's not take those words personally. They aren't rejecting us personally, they are rejecting the service we are offering. Sometimes, it will take several attempts before people are ready to address the issue you can solve, where they finally say Yes!

Have some fun with selling and business. Smile. How do you feel when you do? People like to be with happy people who can provide a little levity. Given the choice, would you rather buy something from someone who made the experience a joy and somewhat fun or from someone who is totally serious? I think most will choose the former. The steel baron, Andrew Carnegie said "There is little success, where there is little laughter". I recall occasions where we were prospecting in pairs and one of us would periodically introduce ourselves as the other, purely unintentional but it made us laugh and of course was a natural ice breaker for the prospect.

Once we had a meeting with a person named (John Jerry or George) Brady. But as a big Tom Brady fan, I said to the sales rep who set the meeting, just a few times, "we're meeting with Tom Brady. We're meeting with TOM BRADY! Whatever you do, don't call the guy Tom!" I did this to get him to laugh a bit. Well as we approached the receptionist, she asked who we were there to see and without hesitation, he said, "We are here to see *Tom Brady*." I immediately started snickering like I was in grade school. He turned and looked over at me with one of those looks your Dad gave you when you were a kid when we did something silly. I had a sinister grin and was doing everything I could to contain composure, but I couldn't keep it in. Live life with joy is what I say! Mr. Brady laughed when we told him the story by the way. Good guy but not a real prospect. Hey, it happens. Not everyone is a prospect. Not even "Tom" Brady!

We really should have some fun in business because sometimes we will lose and that isn't fun. In fact, technically more people will not buy from us than will buy. We will hear more the word No considerably more than Yes in our career. People will choose someone else over us, more than we are chosen. It's OK. We only need the number of clients we agreed upon when we started planning. We just need to learn as much as we can from the losses to help us be better for the next opportunity. Remember that athletes, superstars fail more than they win. The same is true with sales.

How do we feel about people? Do we love them? People need you. You are the best person to serve them if you love them. We should not treat everyone the same. People are different and buy differently. Learning the characteristics and type of person with whom we are serving, will help us to be better at reaching them. The direct buyer does not want numerous options whereas the conscientious person does.

Tell stories. We all like them. Ever since we were tucked in our beds with a bedtime story, we have been programmed to listen to "once upon a time" stories. Can we work on creating a library of stories for different circumstances? When I got started and figured out the value of a story, we could relate a story that the buyer could relate to. Helping people see things from a different viewpoint can often be done with a story.

Let's not forget the need to continue to develop and grow. There is nothing more true than the statement that if we are not growing, we are shrinking. Will you continue to grow and develop? Will you keep honing your people skills? Will you make time each day to learn about people and yourself? Where can you improve and bring more value to the market?

Many of us have improved our situation in life by simply hiring a coach. The coach can help us to reach our full potential. Athletes have coaches. Executives have coaches. People who are serious about their diet and exercise will hire coaches. What about you? Is there a benefit to having a person in your life who cares about you and your growth to become the best version of yourself? That person can help you get to where you want to be in selling with dignity faster as you discuss the intricacies and nuances of sales and people.

Make the Right Choice

The business of selling is changing. Some companies view sales-people as being easily replaceable. I believe buyers would much rather buy from a human with dignity that treats them in a digni-fied way. We will endure. People will make the choice to buy from their friends. As we treat people well, we will be there for them when they are ready to buy.

For a minute I'd like to go back to the lifestyle I lived before I started to master the craft of selling. Financially I was in a posi-tion of being close to the poverty line. Yes, it was a choice I made for careers back then, but still, it was what I became comfortable with economically. I knew it would be easy to get back into clean-ing floors and windows. But I had a better opportunity in front of me.

You have the talent and wherewithal to improve your economic situation. I had to dream bigger and get comfortable with trying out some ideas and concepts that were new to me. Once I did, the economics were substantially different. So many small business owners and salespeople today are not making the income they desire. I am proof that you can reach your goals by making some minor changes by following the guidelines found within these pages.

There is one last item I would like to share with you. We are all faced with choices every day. As we look around us, there are many who have made the choice to sell at all costs with no con-cern for dignity, both for themselves and their customers. The de-cision to sell with dignity is not easy. There will be times that it will appear to be easier to compromise than doing the right thing. Is sacrificing your personal dignity worth a commission check? There will always be more opportunities to serve and sell. Compromising our self-worth and honor will not be worth the price.

Serving others is a way of life. Bringing this service to business is a higher calling. If you choose to sell with dignity, I am confident that you and your business will flourish.

Thank you for reading this book. Now, let's go serve somebody. The selling will follow!

About the Author

 Harry Spaight is a Keynote Speaker, author, and coach. Having grown up in a small New England town with old school values, Harry became involved in mission work. To support himself he had a small janitorial/office cleaning business. The mission work is what gave Harry the most joy and purpose. That work led him to spend two years in the Dominican Republic working with the local population to improve upon their life skills and spiritual growth.

Upon returning to the States, Harry transferred the skills he developed while working with and serving others over to the world of corporate sales. With very little business acumen, Harry applied the principles from the Good Book as to how to treat people. Those two-thousand-year-old principles still proved to be practical. It was all about serving others. Harry believed that people would buy from him if he had a servant's mindset. The principles worked. Harry eventually moved and was leading a team of sales professionals in downtown Washington DC, just a few blocks from 1600 Pennsylvania Ave. Would the principles work in such a competitive market as Washington DC? The answer is yes. The principles are timeless.

Now, after spending over twenty years as an Award-Winning Multi-million Dollar Sales Producer and Sales Leader in the extremely competitive arena of corporate sales, Harry knows firsthand how to be successful in sales and lead winning teams. While many sales leaders choose the cozy corner office, Harry preferred to be in the street, sleeves rolled up so to speak, with his team.

Harry is one who leads by example, knowing it is better to get in the trenches with his people than to bark commands at them. He spearheaded sales teams to achieve the amazing success that resulted in over a hundred million dollars in business. Harry has a "Serve Others First" mindset, which is largely due to having served for over a decade as a missionary.

Harry's understanding of clients, sales professionals, *and* Sales Leaders in building trusting relationships gives people the confidence in putting his knowledge and experience into practice.

Harry is the author of *Selling with Dignity*. He is the co-host of a Top 20 podcast "Lead Sell Grow, The Human Experience".

He works with sales teams and executives to elevate their craft of selling and leading with dignity. Harry can be reached for coaching, consulting, keynotes, and media appearances at Harry@harryspaight.com For updates and more information, please visit www.sellingwithdignity.com